rac
the driving people

Walking the dog
Motorway walks
for drivers and dogs

Lezli Rees

D0583193

Hubble & Hattie

Hubble & Hattie

The Hubble & Hattie imprint was launched in 2009 and is named in memory of two very special Westies owned by Veloce's proprietors.

Since the first book, many more have been added to the list, all with the same underlying objective: to be of real benefit to the species they cover, at the same time promoting compassion, understanding and co-operation between all animals (including human ones!)

Hubble & Hattie is the home of a range of books that cover all-things animal, produced to the same high quality of content and presentation as our motoring books, and offering the same great value for money.

More books from Hubble & Hattie

www.hubbleandhattie.com

First published in March 2011 by Veloce Publishing Limited, Veloce House, Parkway Farm Business Park, Middle Farm Way, Poundbury, Dorchester, Dorset, DT1 3AR, England. Fax 01305 250479/e-mail info@veloce.co.uk/web www.veloce.co.uk or www.velocebooks.com.

ISBN: 978-1-845841-02-7 UPC: 6-36847-04102-1

Contents

introduction

Anyone who drives on the motorways of England, Scotland and Wales will benefit from this guide to walks within 5 miles of motorway exits. All of the UK is covered, from Exeter to Perth and Swansea to Canterbury.

Use this book to get more fun for your fuel, see more of the countryside, take a healthy break, or enjoy a relaxing pub lunch.

Each page features a 30 to 45 minute walk, with a selected pub or café along the way. Activities for children are included, from bouncy castles to nature trails.

All of the walks are suitable for dogs, and those with assistance dogs will find details of accessible paths and disabled facilities – for example, RADAR, a key that is made available to registered disabled people, which enables them to access locked disabled WCs and facilities. The listed pubs all welcome well-behaved canines.

Most of the pubs are traditional inns, serving high quality food at realistic prices. Landlords, chefs and opening times can change quickly, and phone numbers are given for you to check in advance to avoid disappointment.

In the text, 'half-left/right' is a walk direction convention that is used to describe a 45 degree turn in either of these directions.

Many more motorway walks, dog-friendly pubs, beaches and country walks are on our website: www.drivingwithdogs.co.uk. We hope you visit the site and share your comments and suggestions.

From London to Leeds, via Leicester and Sheffield

Junction	
5	Aldenham Country Park
10	Stockwood Park & Discovery Centre
11	Dunstable Downs Country Park
12	Sundon Hills
14	Broughton Grounds Community Woodlands
15	Salcey Forest
18	Crick
20	Walcote
22	Billa Barra Hill Nature Reserve
23A	Donington Services (northbound)
25	Elvaston Country Park
27	Linby Trail
Tibshelf Services	Five Pits Trail
29	Rowthorne Walk
31	Rother Valley Country Park
34	Scholes Coppice
35	Wentworth
37	Cannon Hall Park
38	Yorkshire Sculpture Park
39	Pugneys Country Park
46	Temple Newsam

walking THE DOG

M1 Junction 5

Aldenham Country Park WD6 3AT

Getting there
From Junction 5 take the A41 Harrow, northbound exit 1, southbound exit 2. At roundabout take exit 2, Central London A41, past a McDonalds on the left. At the next roundabout take exit 1, Aldenham Country Park. Turn left, Aldenham Road. Turn left to the car park.

Return to M1 Junction 5
Turn right from car park, Aldenham Road. Continue to the A41 junction and turn left, Aylesbury. At the roundabout take exit 2, A41 signed M1 and return to the motorway.

The walk
For a 30-40 minute stroll, walk through the car park away from the adventure playground and farm, following signs to Hundred Acre Wood, haunt of Winnie the Pooh. The Pooh Bear theme expands and you can

visit the 'homes' of Kanga, Eeyore and Wol. There's an enclosed paddock for dogs to run free.

A longer, 40-60 minute circular Lakeside Walk starts from the refreshment kiosk.

The urban farm is well worth a visit – with or without children – to see farmyard favourites, including an enormous grinning sow, leaping goats, shire horses, and rare-breed sheep.

Facilities
Car park charge on exit, coins only. WC. Refreshment kiosk; picnic area. Wheelchair access. Adventure playground, urban farm. Campervan access.

Getting there

Leave the M1 at Junction 10 for Junction 10A, following the motorway arm until its end, then follow signs to Stockwood Country Park.

For the Discovery Centre and facilities, turn left at the tourist sign for the car park.

For the park only, turn left at the Country Park signpost after the Golf Club – White Hill Avenue.

Turn left at the T-junction at the end; the car park entrance is soon after on the left.

Return to M1 Junction 10

From the Discovery Centre return to the main road and turn right. Continue to the roundabout at Junction 10A, and rejoin the M1 (north or south).

The walk

An ideal walk for keeping your feet dry on wet days, as the paths are hard-surfaced, and friendly to buggy wheels and wheelchairs.

There's no shortage of canine interest, either, with old trees, plenty of squirrels, and lots of room for ball games.

Facilities

There are several car parks for park users, and a separate car park for the museum. All are free. If you're planning a visit to the museum/Discovery Centre as well as doing the dog walk, it's okay to park in the museum car park (London Road) so that you're nearer to the facilities.

Entry to the Discovery Centre is free. Inside, there are WCs, including disabled facilities. Café. Shop. Children's activities. Gardens, and exhibitions. Summer opening hours are: 1000-1700 Mon-Friday; 1100-1700 weekends. Winter: 1000-1600 Monday-Friday, 1100-1600 weekends.

Dunstable Downs Country Park LU6 2GY

Getting there

From Junction 11 take the A505, Dunstable; northbound exit 1, southbound exit 3. At the next roundabout take exit 2, Dunstable A505. Pass a BP garage on the left and a retail park (with Sainsbury and McDonalds) to the right. In Dunstable, follow signs to Aston Clinton B489, over 3 mini roundabouts. At the next roundabout turn left – Whipsnade B4541 – and continue to the Dunstable Downs car park on the right. The second car park is closer to the facilities and café.

Return to M1 Junction 11

Turn left from the car park then turn right, signed B489 Dunstable. Stay on the B489 through Dunstable and continue straight as the B489 becomes the A505, signed M1 and Luton.

The walk

At the visitor centre enjoy the view from this astonishing vantage point overlooking the Chiltern Valley.

The walk follows part of the Icknield Way, an ancient track that was the pre-Roman highway between the Ivinghoe Beacon in Hertfordshire and Norfolk. It's one of the oldest known routes in Britain (there's more detail on the notice board). Follow the clearly-signed path and turn round to return at your halfway point.

Facilities

P&D car park (free to National Trust members). WC+disabled. Visitor centre. Café. Shop. Campervan access.

Getting there

From Junction 12 follow signs to Flitwick/Woburn A5120. At the roundabout take exit 2, Harlington Station. Pass the railway station. At the crossroads turn right, past The Carpenters Arms, and continue to the brow of the hill where the car park is on the left.

Return to M1 Junction 12

Turn right out of the car park. Turn left at the crossroads just after The Carpenters Arms. Pass Harlington Station on the left, and then turn left onto Toddington Road. At the roundabout take exit 1, A5120 Harlington Road, and rejoin the motorway.

The walk

Sundon Hills is one of the highest points in Bedfordshire, with stunning views over the county and the Sharpenhoe Clappers. The long distance John Bunyan Trail passes through the park. There are no marked paths, but the rolling hills are grassy and straightforward to navigate. It's easy to see why Sundon Hills is part of the Chilterns Area of Outstanding Natural Beauty.

Facilities

Free parking. Wheelchair access. Picnic tables. Campervan access. The Carpenters Arms (01525 872384). Lunch from 1200 (except Mondays). Well-behaved dogs are welcome in the bar.

Broughton Grounds Community Woodlands

Getting there
From Junction 14, take the A509, Milton Keynes. At the next roundabout take the A5130, Woburn Sands/Wavendon. Turn left, signed Gravel Quarry/Broughton Grounds Lane – no through road. Pass a riding school on the right, go over the motorway and the entrance to the small car park is on the left on a right-hand corner.

Return to M1 Junction 14
Retrace your route, turning right at the end of Broughton Grounds Lane.

The walk
From the car park take the track on the right, through a gate, and continue until you see a yellow waymark. Follow the arrow direction into the field ahead. About halfway across the field turn right and pass a pond to the left. Continue to the waymarked footbridge and stile and then turn half-right into a young wood. At a crossing of paths, continue straight on til you come to a gate; there's a fishing lake on the right. Follow the path along the left side of the field and back to the car park.

In the woodland section you may well see Muntjac deer. These are the smallest deer in the UK, and not aggressive.

Facilities
Free parking. Campervan access.

Getting there

From Junction 15 take the A508, Stony Stratford at the first roundabout, and then exit 2 at the next roundabout. Enter Roade and turn left onto Northampton Road. Pass a school on the left and turn left, signed Hartwell. Drive though Hartwell. At the crossroads turn left, signed Quinton, Northampton. Salcey Forest car park is on the right.

Return to M1 Junction 15

Turn left from the car park, and then right, signed Hartwell. Continue through Hartwell village to enter Roade. At the T-junction turn right, signed Northampton. At the next T-junction turn right, signed M1 (A508).

The walk

Salcey Forest is what remains of a former royal forest, and contains ancient oak trees known as 'druids' that are said to be over 500 years old. A keen eye can still recognise signs of ancient wood banks and buildings.

There are three marked trails through the woods on well maintained paths. The first is 0.75 mile in length, and is suitable for wheelchair users. The second trail is 1.5 miles, and the third is 6 miles.

There's plenty for all the family to do, including a tree-top walk.

Facilities

P&D gated car park, closes 1900 in summer. WC. Café. Children's play area. Campervan access.

Crick NN6 7TX

Getting there
From Junction 18 take the turning signed 'Dept of Transport Weighbridge.' At first roundabout take exit 3, Yelvertoft, Crick. At the next roundabout take exit 1 Crick, Yelvertoft. Enter Crick. Drive to the top of the hill and park near the Red Lion on the right.

Return to M1 Junction 18
Leave the Red Lion and take exit 2 at the roundabout. At the next roundabout take exit 1, A428, Rugby, and rejoin the motorway at the next roundabout.

The walk
From the Red Lion turn left. Pass the High Street turning and go down the hill. Turn left at The Derry. At the footpath arrows, bear right. Cross a stile and follow the arrow uphill to another post. Take a half left to carry on over the brow of the hill. Head for a black arrow to the right of a tree and then cross a wooden footbridge and stile into the next field.

Head slightly to the left up the hill. Climb a stile to the left of a tree to an arrow pointing half left. Over the hill aim for a gap in the far left corner of the field and walk through to the next field. Take in the view and then turn and retrace your steps.

Facilities
Food and snacks are available at the 17th century Red Lion (01788 822342). Dogs are allowed in the bar and beer garden. Campervan access.

Getting there
From Junction 20 take the A304, Market Harborough. Enter Walcote and park at The Tavern Inn on the left.

Return to M1 Junction 20
Turn right out of the car park onto the A4304, which leads directly back to the M1 Junction 20.

The walk
Turn right from the car park and walk to a footpath sign on the other side of the road. Turn right at the gateway of number 5, through the garden and the wooden gate and stile on the other side. Follow an arrow pointing slightly to the right along the bottom of a field. Climb a stile and follow the arrow straight on. Turn left after a children's play area to follow the bridleway to Misterton. Stay on the bridleway through a gate and into a field. Bear left to join a farm track. The track becomes a surfaced lane and crosses a stream. This is the outskirts of Misterton village, with a church on the right. Turn around here to retrace the route to Walcote.

Facilities
Food is served from 1200 at The Tavern Inn, Walcote (01455 553338). Dogs welcome at the outdoor tables. Petrol station in village.

Campervan access.

walking THE DOG

Billa Barra Hill Nature Reserve

Getting there
From Junction 22 take the A511, Ashby, Coalville. Pass a BP service station. At the roundabout take exit 1, Stanton, Thornton. Pass Markfield Equestrian Centre on the left. Turn right, signed Local Nature Reserve, Billa Barra Lane. Take the first right turn for the National Forest car park.

Return to M1 Junction 22
Turn left from the car park. Turn left at the T-junction and continue to a roundabout. Take exit 2 to rejoin the M1.

The walk
Go through the kissing gate at the back of the car park and walk up the hill. Follow the path as it bears to the right beside the Charnwood Noon Column.

Continue towards the trees and gorse bushes, ignoring a path crossing yours. Bear right between holly trees, then bear half left along the clearly trodden path towards the top of the hill, passing through a gap in the hedgerow. Continue on with a dry stone wall to the left to the very top of the mound. Walk down the other side and you'll be able to see the car park at the bottom.

Facilities
None on walk. BP service station on A511 with Burger King, Little Chef, petrol and WC. Campervan access.

Getting there

Follow signs to Donington Services from Junction 23A.

Return to M1 Northbound

Follow the signs to return to the M1 via the A453.

The walk

This is one of the gateways to the National Forest, with an interpretation board near the services entrance explaining the project.

Keeping the services block on your left, follow a path round to the start of a grassy area. Walk forward, bearing slightly right, to join a path running parallel to one of the service roads. Follow this path to the public footpath sign, and then turn left.

At this point, the walk becomes properly rural as the path leads downhill between tilled fields, and the sounds of the motorway give way to birdsong. Follow the path for 20 minutes or so, then turn and retrace your steps to the car park.

Facilities

Moto service station. Dogs on leads may be taken to the outside tables. Campervan access.

Elvaston Country Park DE72 3EP

Getting there
From Junction 25 take the A52, Derby; northbound exit 1, southbound exit 4. Enter Borrowash and turn left, Victoria Avenue. At a T-junction turn right. At the next T-junction turn left, then immediately right, Station Road. Turn right at the brown signpost to Elvaston Country Park. This is also the Derby Showground, and is busy on major show days.

Return to M1 Junction 25
Leave the car park and turn left. Enter Borrowash. Turn left onto the A6005, signed Derby. Enter Spondon. At the roundabout, take the 2nd exit, at the next roundabout take the 3rd exit, signed M1, to return to the motorway.

The walk

To join the trails, turn left from the rear of the car park to cross the bridge. A left turn takes you through a majestic avenue of Cedars of Lebanon to approach the 'castle' (which is more of a stately home) on a broad, grassy approach. The café, visitor centre, and shop lie in the courtyard.

There are more than 200 acres of woodland and formal gardens here, so there are many trail options to choose from, all starting from the central courtyard.

Facilities
P&D car park. WC+disabled. Café. Shop. Visitor centre. Easy-access trails. Children's playground. Nature trails. Free dog poo bags from car park kiosk. Campervan access.

Getting there

From Junction 27 take the A608/A611 signed Hucknall, crossing two roundabouts. At the traffic lights continue towards Hucknall. At the next two roundabouts take exit 1, Linby B6011. After a railway crossing, enter Linby and park in The Horse and Groom car park on the left.

Return to M1 Junction 27

Turn right from the car park and take exit 2, Mansfield, at the roundabout. At the next roundabout, take exit 3 signed Mansfield, M1, and follow signs to return to the motorway.

The walk

With your back to the Horse and Groom, turn right past the war memorial and at the roundabout turn right at a wooden public footpath sign. This is the Linby Trail, a straight, wide path running alongside a brook. After a mile or so the trail divides and the path on the right continues up a small hill to the gatehouse of Newstead Abbey, sometime home of the poet Lord Byron. Reverse the route to return to Linby.

Facilities

The Horse and Groom (0115 963 2219), food and snacks available, roasts on Sundays. Children's play area. Well-behaved dogs permitted in the bar area and garden seating. Campervan access.

Five Pits Trail DE55 5TZ

Getting there
Leave the M1 and park at Tibshelf Services.

Return to M1
Return to the M1 from the services as signed.

The walk
Southbound services. Head up the bank from the services vehicle entrance and turn left at the top to follow a trodden path to a fence. Cross the fence and turn left onto a surfaced path and over the motorway bridge. Stay on this path, ignoring other turnings, to the entrance to the trails.

Northbound services. Walk towards the motel and exit on the service road. Turn right, and walk a few yards to a house before a bridge. Turn right here onto a track. Turn left and walk downhill to a bike barrier and the start of the trails.

Both routes now reach a waymark, which shows paths branching off in every possible direction. Turn right onto the Five Pits Trail, just one of many fine walking routes here.

Facilities
RoadChef motorway services, northbound and southbound. Campervan access.

Getting there

From Junction 29 take the A6175, Clay Cross, Hardwick Hall; northbound exit 1, southbound exit 4. Turn left signed Stainsby, Hardwick Hall and Stainsby Mill. Drive under the M1, and take the second left turn signed Hardwick Inn. Park in the overspill car park on the right before the inn.

Return to M1 Junction 29

Reverse your route; the motorway is clearly signed.

The walk

Walk past the pub, around a cattle grid and uphill along the lane. At a footpath sign bear right through a wooden gate. Follow the grassy track straight ahead, through a gate and uphill to a purple waymark for the 'Hardwick Rowthorne Walk.' At the top there's a National Trust board showing the routes of the many walks here. The path to the left leads to Hardwick Hall (no dogs). Turn right to walk through the woodland (Lady Spencer's Walk).

For a shorter walk, you may decide to forego the marked trails and just enjoy pottering in the woodland.

Facilities

Hardwick Inn (01246 850245). A 15th century coaching inn providing snacks and meals, and a very large garden; food available from 1200; dogs welcome outside, water buckets provided. Campervan access.

walking THE DOG

Rother Valley Country Park S26 5PQ

Getting there
From Junction 31 take the A57 Sheffield; northbound exit 1, southbound exit 3. At the roundabout take exit 1, A618 signed Rother Valley Country Park. Turn right into the car park.

Return to M1 Junction 31
Exit the park and turn left. At the roundabout take exit 2, A57 Worksop, and return to the M1.

The walk
This 750 acre country park has a number of trails and strolling areas. It's also a stunningly brilliant way of making positive use of the town's flood defences – which is what this park is all about. A network of footpaths is clearly signed from the visitor centre, near the WCs and children's activities.

Dog walkers tend to park in one of the earlier lakeside car parks and take circular routes around the lakes. The first lake, and the smallest, is the Northern Lake which can be circumnavigated in 45 minutes or so. The Rother Valley Lake is the largest one, and is a much longer walk.

Facilities
Several large car parks; entry charge includes parking, closes at dusk. WC+disabled. Café. Shops. Visitor centre. Craft centre. PlayDales for children. Campervan access.

Getting there

Northbound traffic: leave the M1 at Junction 34 and take exit 3 signed Rotherham A631, M1 (north). At the next roundabout take exit 5, Rotherham A6109. Southbound traffic: leave the M1 at Junction 34 and take exit 2 Rotherham A6109.

Both routes: continue ahead to a roundabout and take exit 1 signed Huddersfield A629. Just before the village of Thorpe Hesley, turn right signed Scholes (at the Sportsman pub). Continue on this lane to Scholes. The Bay Horse is on the right.

Return to M1 Junction 34

Turn left from the car park. At the crossroads turn left. At the roundabout, take exit 3, M1. At the next roundabout, follow the signs to the M1.

The walk

Turn left from the car park and then turn left at a public footpath sign along a driveway. This brings you into Scholes Coppice.

Walk over the footbridge as far as a fork in the path to the footpath signs. The 45 minute circular walk is clearly marked with yellow arrows.

A slight, signed detour leads to an interpretation board explaining the Iron Age history of the coppice.

Facilities

The Bay Horse (0114 2468085) is a traditional inn, with a good selection of hearty bar snacks and meals, and a roaring fire in winter. Meals available weekends from 1200, weekdays from 1700. Well-behaved dogs on leads welcome in the rear bar. Campervan access.

Wentworth S62 7TF

Getting there
Leave the M1 at Junction 35 and take the A629, Rotherham, northbound 3, southbound exit 1. Enter Thorpe Hesley.

Turn left onto the B6086, signed Hoyland, Wentworth (Upper Wortley Road). At the mini roundabout, take the 2nd exit (Thorpe Street). Continue along this lane. Before entering Wentworth, turn right into the Wentworth Garden Centre car park.

Return to M1 Junction 35
Turn left out of the car park. At the mini roundabout, take exit 1. At the T-junction turn right and continue to rejoin the M1.

The walk
A large field next to the car park is ideal for immediate dog relief and off-lead games. After that, there's a delightful short walk through the historic gardens, and a clearly-signed footpath for a stroll from the garden centre into the Wentworth Estate and back.

Facilities
Free parking. WCs+disabled. Courtyard café/delicatessen and shops. Large pet shop.

Getting there

From Junction 37 take the A628, Manchester. At the next roundabout take exit 3, Manchester A628, and at the following roundabout take exit 1, Manchester A628. At the next roundabout take exit 2 and bear right to Higham Lane. Continue onto Higham Common Road and turn left at the traffic lights, A635. Turn right, Bark House Lane, at a tourist sign for Cannon Hall Country Park, then turn right to the park.

Return to M1 Junction 37

Turn left from the car park, and at the T-junction turn left signed Barnsley A635. At the traffic lights turn right, signed Dodworth. Thereafter, follow signs for Barnsley A628 to reach the M1 interchange.

The walk

There's little chance of getting lost in this 70 acre expanse of largely flat and open parkland. Stroll alongside the small river from the car park, then strike out into the park on a broad path. Follow the path on a circular orbit for a 30-40 minute walk.

If you have time, the historic walled garden next to the Hall is worth a visit. Quaffers of Australian wine will be intrigued to know that a cutting from a vine cultivated here was exported to Australia in 1802, and its offspring form the roots of today's Ozzie wine industry.

Facilities

P&D car park. WC+disabled. Café with fresh cakes and home-made soup.

walking THE DOG

Yorkshire Sculpture Park WF4 4LG

Getting there
From Junction 38 take the A637, Huddersfield. Continue, ignoring a car park on the left. At a roundabout turn left at the brown tourist sign for Sculpture Park.

Return to M1 Junction 38
Turn right out of the park onto the A637 and rejoin the M1 at the next roundabout.

The walk
This walk lies in the Yorkshire Sculpture Park, an outdoor art gallery. The gallery reception desk has maps of the park and sculptures.

Start from the gate by the gallery to follow the path downhill towards the lake. Bear left at the foot of the slope to walk with the lake on your right. Turn right through a gate onto Dam Head bridge, to join the marked Longside Route around the perimeter of the park in a full circle past the Longside gallery. Turn right after the bridge, keeping the lake on your right, to return to the car park. Watch out for territorial geese!

Facilities
P&D car park. Open 1000-1800. WC+disabled. Café (dogs outside only). Gallery shop. Free walks leaflets. Campervan access.

Pugneys Country Park WF2 7EQ

Getting there
From Junction 39 take the A636, Wakefield. At the roundabout take exit 2, A636 Wakefield. At the next roundabout take exit 3 into Pugneys Country Park.

Return to M1 Junction 39
Leave the park, take exit 2 at the roundabout, Denby Dale A636/M1. At the next roundabout, take exit 2 signed M1/A636 to return to the M1.

The walk
The main purpose of this park is to encourage watersports in the area, and two fine lakes and a nature reserve have been created from the sites of former quarries and open cast mines.

A surfaced and accessible 1.6 mile circular path runs around the larger lake, ideal for a 45 minute walk. It can be quite exciting to watch the dinghy sailors and surfers in training on a windy day as you walk.

Facilities
Free parking for first hour. Car park 0900-2130. WC. Café, picnic tables. Children's play area. Petrol station on the A636. Campervan access.

walking THE DOG

Temple Newsam LS15 0AE

Getting there

From Junction 46 take the A63, Leeds. At the next roundabout take exit 3, A6120, ring road. Follow the A6120 at the next roundabout. At the third roundabout take exit 2, A63 and Temple Newsam House. At the traffic lights turn left signed Temple Newsam House, Colton Road. Go straight over a mini roundabout into Temple Newsam.

Return to M1 Junction 46

Leave the Lodge car park and turn left to return on Colton Road to the traffic lights on the Selby Road. Turn right (A63) and then take exit 2 at the roundabout, signed M1.

The walk

With over 1500 acres of woodland and parkland, there is plenty of walking choice. There are thirty distinct woods within the grounds, as well as a number of different gardens.

From the house, a pleasant circular walk goes past Little Temple to Wilderness Wood, onward to Coppice Wood and back to the house via Pegasus Wood.

Dog walkers may prefer to start at the Lodge car park, and walk over the gently undulating velvet green grass towards the house, and then into the woods.

Facilities

The Lodge car park (free). House car park P&D. Visitor centre (0113 264 7321). WC+disabled. Tea rooms. Shop. Campervan access.

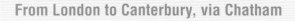

M2

From London to Canterbury, via Chatham

Junction

1	Shorne Wood (westbound)
2	Ranscombe Park Nature Reserve
3	Syle Wood
4	Capstone Farm Country Park
5	Oad Street
6	Perry Wood
7	Dargate Wood

Shorne Wood DA12 3HX   Westbound only

Getting there
From Junction 1 continue onto the A2. Take the Cobham, Shorne exit, and then exit 1 at a roundabout – Brewers Road. Continue ahead, then turn left into Shorne Wood Country Park.

Return to A2 westbound
Turn right out of the car park, and at the roundabout take exit 4, signed London M25, to rejoin the A2 westbound.

The walk
Shorne Wood comprises over 170 acres of ancient woodland and heath, water meadows, and lakes. It was formerly part of the Cobham Estate.

There are several colour-coded paths and circular walks that take you around the park. A footpath leaflet is available at the information centre.

The Woodland Track, which starts at the visitor centre, provides a very dog-centric walk. There's a sign pointing to Shorne Cam pool – a designated venue for doggy-paddling!

Facilities
P&D parking. WC+disabled. Visitor centre. Café. Shop. Picnic area. Sensory garden. Adventure playground. Electro-scooter hire (book on 01474 823800). Campervan access.

Getting there
From Junction 2 take the A228, Rochester, West Malling. At the next roundabout take exit 2 signed M20, West Malling. The small car park for Ranscombe Park is immediately on the right.

Return to M2 Junction 2
Leave the car park, turn left and join the motorway at the roundabout.

The walk
Several trails are indicated by yellow waymarks, and the North Downs Way also passes through the park. As soon as you walk around the corner from the car park, the noise and fumes of the traffic drop away, and the sense of space and quiet is amazing.

   Walk 1: Proceed to the first waymark on the right, turn left, and follow the path as it leads away from the railway line (fenced), and into the peace and tranquillity of rural Kent.

   Walk 2: Proceed to the second waymark and select a trail to follow past the rape fields and into a secluded open valley beyond.

Facilities
Free car park. Campervan access.

walking THE DOG

Syle Wood ME5 9RJ

Getting there
From Junction 3 take the A229, Maidstone, Chatham. At the Lord Lees
roundabout take exit 3, A229 Chatham, Rochester. After half a mile turn
left, signed Blue Bell Hill. Turn right into Common Road and park at The
Robin Hood pub on the right.

Return to M2 Junction 3
Retrace the route to the A229, and turn left. At the roundabout take exit
4, signed London M2, to rejoin the motorway.

The walk
Return to the road and turn left. At a footpath sign walk left across a
field and head into the trees. After this, the path is straight and heads
gently downhill. Ignore all tracks to the left and right. Emerge from the
wood and turn left onto a signed bridleway just before Upper Nathenden
Farm. This path returns directly to The Robin Hood garden on a slight
upward incline. Allow an hour for this 2.5 mile walk.

Facilities
At The Robin Hood (01634 861500), pub food is available 1200-1430.
Big play area for children. Dogs are welcome in the bar and spacious
garden seating area. Campervan access.

Getting there

From Junction 4 take the A278, signed Gillingham. At the next roundabout take exit 2, Rainham A278, and at the second roundabout take exit 2, Gillingham A2. Stay on the A2 across two more roundabouts. Turn left, signed Capstone Country Park. Go down the hill and take exit 1 at a mini roundabout. At the second roundabout take exit 2, Capstone Farm Country Park. The car park is on the right.

Return to M2 Junction 4

Turn left from the car park and left again (Almond Grove). Turn left again (Chapel Lane) and then right (Hempstead Valley Drive). At the roundabout, take exit 1 (Sharsted Way). At the next roundabout take exit 3 A278, signed London, Dover M2 to return to the motorway.

The walk

This popular, 280 acre park has several paths and trails. Join the main footpath, which runs parallel to the larger section of the car park. Where the path goes slightly uphill, ignore a turning to the left and keep straight on through the Millennium Wood. Turn left at the far edge of Orchid Wood to skirt around Capstone Wood. Pass through Round Glade and return to the car park through the Millennium Wood.

Facilities

Free car park, closes at dusk. WC+disabled. Café. Visitor centre with maps (1000-1630). Children's play area. Campervan access.

Oad Street ME9 8LB

Getting there

Leave the M2 at Junction 5 signed Sittingbourne, Channel Tunnel. At a roundabout take exit 4, A249 Maidstone. Turn left at a signpost to Bredgar, Tunstall (Pett Lane). Park at either The Plough and Harrow or the craft centre car park.

Return to M2 Junction 5

Turn right out of the craft centre car park. At a T-junction turn left, signed Maidstone. At the next T-junction turn right. At the next junction turn left, signed M2/M20, to return to the motorway.

The walk

Turn right from the craft centre, or cross the road from The Plough and Harrow, and walk down the lane to a footpath sign on the left. Climb the stile and walk through a field with the hedge to your right, and a lovely view of a traditional oast house to the left.

At the corner of the field follow the path round to the right and over another stile. Turn left and immediately right to walk between well-fenced horse paddocks. Go through the gate ahead and walk down towards the stables. Just after the stables keep a sharp eye out for a rickety stile to the left. Climb this stile and walk uphill to another stile. Turn right and walk with

the fence on your right until the next (and final) stile. Carry straight on through a wooden kissing gate into a small, rabbit-filled wood beyond. Retrace your route to return.

Facilities

At The Plough and Harrow (01795 843351); open all day. Bar snacks and meals, log fire in winter. Well-behaved dogs on leads are welcome in the bar. At the craft centre: WC, tearoom, shop. Campervan access.

Getting there

Leave the M2 at Junction 6 and take the A251, Ashford. Drive through North Street. Turn left, signed Selling, New House Lane. Stay on this lane, passing through Hogben's Hill, following signs to Selling. Drive through Selling. Pass Norham Farm on the left, and take the first right turn, signed Perry Wood and The Rose and Crown. At the crossroads turn left, signed Perry Wood car park, and the car park is on the left.

Return to M2 Junction 6

Turn right out of the car park and right again. At the T-junction turn left and drive through Selling. Continue through Hogben's Hill. Pass Newhouse Farm on the left and turn right – A251 – at the crossroads. Continue on the A251 to rejoin the M2.

The walk

There are two boards with walking information, and clearly-signed paths through this enchanting wood.

Yellow arrows direct walkers on a short, circular walk through an avenue of rhododendron and beech trees.

Perry Wood is a charming place to walk and think, with little trace of modern life.

Facilities

Free parking. The 18th century White Lion (01227 752211) in nearby Selling (ME13 9RQ) welcomes children and dogs. Bar/restaurant food available. Campervan access.

Dargate Wood ME13 9HB

Getting there
At Junction 7 continue on the A299. Branch left, signed Dargate. Turn left into High Street Road. Turn left and then right onto Plum Pudding Lane, and park at The Dove on the left.

Return to M2 Junction 7
Turn right from the car park, Plum Pudding Lane. After half a mile turn left. Take the next left and then merge onto the A299 to return to the M2 (London).

The walk
With The Dove behind you, walk to a Public Bridleway sign just after Elm Tree Cottage.

Follow the path as it winds uphill into the woods, and look back to enjoy the fabulous view of the Thames Estuary and sea beyond.

The path is waymarked with blue posts, and is easy to follow. In spring, the wood is full of rabbits, squirrels, and birdsong.

Turn around to return to The Dove at a halfway point of your choosing.

Facilities
The Dove (01227 751360) is a quaint, Victorian country pub with marvellous food. Children are welcome. Dogs are allowed in the bar and garden area.

From London to Southampton, via Bracknell and Winchester

Junction

3	Lightwater Country Park
4	Basingstoke Canal Centre
5	Hook Common
6	Basing Lime Pit
9	Easton
10	St Catherine's Hill
12	Otterbourne Park Wood

walking THE DOG

Lightwater Country Park GU18 5RG

Getting there
Leave the M3 at Junction 3 and take the A322, Guildford. At the roundabout get in the right-hand lane for the A322 Guildford exit, and almost immediately take a sliproad to the right, signed Lightwater Country Park. Turn right at the tourist sign to Lightwater Country Park, The Avenue. The entrance to the park is at the end of the road.

Return to M3 Junction 3
Leave the park along The Avenue. Turn right at the T-junction on to the dual carriageway, and at the roundabout rejoin the M3.

The walk
Circular trails of varying lengths begin at the visitor centre, each featuring a different aspect of the park. The paths are surfaced, and fully accessible.

The Lakeside walk is the shortest, and gradient-free. The Nature trail, marked with numbered posts, is a 40 minute walk. The Heathland Trail is longer, with stunning views over the heathland. Maps of all the trails are available from the visitor centre.

Facilities
Free parking. WC+disabled. Refreshments at the leisure centre. Children's play area. Campervan access.

Basingstoke Canal Centre GU16 6DD

Getting there
From Junction 4 take the A331 Guildford, Farnborough. Continue on this road until you come to a branch to the left, signed Mytchett. The Basingstoke Canal Centre is well signed from here.

Return to M3 Junction 4
Turn right from the car park and drive straight over the mini roundabout, Coleford Bridge Road. Turn left at a mini roundabout, signed Farnborough Park. At the next roundabout, take exit 2 and merge with the A331, signed M3, to rejoin the motorway.

The walk
If it's flat walking you're after, then a towpath stroll is ideal. Cross the bridge to the less crowded path, and turn left or right as the fancy takes you. The 32 mile towpath is a Site of Special Scientific Interest nature reserve, and a great place for spotting wildlife.

Facilities
Free parking 0930 to 2200. Café. WC. Children's play area. Picnic area. Gift shop. Visitor centre. Canoe and pedalo hire, boat trips, and a floating art gallery.

walking THE DOG

Hook Common RG27 9JJ

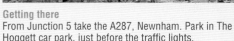

Getting there
From Junction 5 take the A287, Newnham. Park in The
Hoggett car park, just before the traffic lights.

Return to M3 Junction 5
Turn left out of the car park onto the A287 and back to the motorway.

The walk
From the car park, cross to Holly Bush Lane. Walk past the
immaculately kept mobile homes on the left, and enter the common
proper. The woodland path is quite narrow, but easy to follow as it
winds through the old trees with their carpeting of bracken. There is
only one small path so you won't get lost here. Walk until the trees
begin to thin out and then bear left on the track to stay on the common.
Retrace your route to return to The Hoggett.

Facilities
At the Hoggett (01256 763009). Lunch 1200-1400. Friday breakfast
0730-0900. Dogs are welcome in the bar and at the outside tables.
Campervan access.

Getting there

From Junction 6, northbound take exit 1; southbound exit 2 at the roundabout. At the next roundabout take exit 3, Old Basing. Immediately turn left signed Basing Lime Pits (one way). Park in either of the two car parks on the right; the first is better for children.

Return to M3 Junction 6

Turn right out of either car park. At the T-junction turn right, The Street, and then immediately turn right again, Brown Lane. At the traffic lights turn right, Park Lane. At the T-junction turn right, London Road. At the roundabout take exit 3 signed M3/London/South West to rejoin the motorway.

The walk

The two car parks are close together, and the walk starts from the top of the natural amphitheatre. Head uphill towards the left-hand corner. There is a squeezer stile to the left of a dog bin which leads through onto common land beyond. This is a large, flat area which can be walked around in 25 minutes.

Facilities

Free parking. Children's play area and adventure playground by the first car park. Fitness trail. Campervan access.

Refreshments at the 16th century Crown Inn (01256 321424) just a few moments away in Old Basing village. To save time you can phone your menu choices through in advance and have a meal waiting for you on arrival. Well-behaved dogs on leads are welcome in parts of the bar and the garden.

walking THE DOG

Easton SO21 1EJ

Getting there
From Junction 9 take the A272, Winchester, northbound exit 4; southbound exit 1. At the roundabout, take exit 1, A31 Alvesford, Alton. At the next roundabout follow signs to Easton, on Castle Lane. Enter Easton and continue to a T-junction. Park in The Cricketers Inn car park.

Return to M3 Junction 9
Turn left from the car park and immediately right onto Castle Lane. At the roundabout take exit 2, signed M3. At the next roundabout take exit 2 signed M3 to rejoin the motorway.

The walk
From the car park, cross the road and follow signs for St Mary's church. Pass the lychgate and look for the shell logo of the Pilgrim's Way, a long-distance path from Winchester to Canterbury. Just after the Old Schoolhouse turn right, and then immediately left to a footpath sign. Cross the football pitch diagonally and go through a kissing gate in a clump of trees in the corner.

Now follow the clear path with the River Itchen to your right, continuing in this direction in a field-stile-field pattern until your halfway point. Turn around to return with the river to the left. Water-loving dogs will adore this walk!

Facilities
At The Cricketers Inn (01962 779353), food is served from midday. Dogs are welcome in the public bar and outside tables. Campervan access.

Getting there
From Junction 10 take exit 1 at the roundabout signed St Catherine's P&R, Garnier Way. Drive over a small railway bridge and park in the car park immediately on the left, just before a bridge over the river.

Return to M3 Junction 10
Leave the car park and turn right. At the roundabout take exit 2. At the next roundabout take exit 2 signed M3 London, Basingstoke, to return to the motorway.

The walk
Walk with the river on your right and continue for about 15 minutes until the path opens out, and you reach an interpretation board at the entrance to St Catherine's Hill.

A long set of steps leads to the top – and a splendid view of Winchester. The hill has been purposefully used for around 3000 years, with traces of Iron Age defences, as well as a Norman chapel. It's a great place for a picnic on a sunny day.

This walk can also be continued alongside the river on a flat path if you want to skip the steps.

Turn around to return to the car park, with the river on the left.

Facilities
Free car park. Campervan access.

walking THE DOG

Otterbourne Park Wood SO21 2HW

Getting there
From Junction 12 follow the sign to Chandlers Ford. At a mini roundabout, take exit 2, Otterbourne Hill. Turn right onto Boyatt Lane, left onto Park Lane, and park.

Return to M3 Junction 12
Turn, and turn right at the end of Park Lane. At the T-junction turn right, Boyatt Lane. Pass The Otter on the left and turn left at the crossroads, Otterbourne Hill. At the roundabout take exit 1 to return to the M3.

The walk
Enter Otterbourne Park Wood on the signed footpath. This leads downhill on the outward leg of the walk, and uphill on the return section.

There are also many paths to the sides, and this is an enchanting place to ramble in at will.

Otterbourne Park Wood is a Heritage Site, with gnarled ancient oak trees and traces of an old Roman road from Winchester.

Facilities
Free parking. The Otter (0238 0252685) serves food, and is family- and dog-friendly. Campervan access.

M4

From London to South Wales, via Reading and Bristol

Junction

4	Harmondsworth Moor
7	Jubilee River
13	Chieveley Services
15	Coate Water
16	Lydiard Park
17	Kington St Michael
24	Caerleon
27	Monmouth & Brecon Canal
28	Tredegar House
30	Coed Coesau Whips, Cardiff Gate Services
32	Castell Coch
33	St Fagans Walk
34	Tyn-y-Coed Forest
36	Bryngarw
37	Kenfig Dunes
40	Afon Argoed Forest
45	Cwm Clydach
46	Felindre

Harmondsworth Moor UB7 0AQ

Getting there

From the Junction 4 exit roundabout take the A408, Uxbridge, and follow signs for 'All other routes.' Shortly, take the first left, signed Harmondsworth. At the next roundabout take exit 2, A3044, Harmondsworth. Continue over a mini roundabout and enter Harmondsworth. At the next mini roundabout take exit 2, Harmondsworth High Street. Park in the free bays on the High Street.

Return to M4 Junction 4

Leave Harmondsworth on the High Street and take exit 2 at the mini roundabout. At the next mini roundabout take exit 2, signed M4. At the roundabout take exit 2 and return to the motorway as signed.

The walk

Start from Moor Lane to the left of The Five Bells pub, and walk to a public footpath sign. Cross the bridge and turn right to enter an enclosed park – Harmondsworth Moor – which has benefited from some creative park management.

Beyond the landscaped section and large adventure playground, stiles and gates lead into the surrounding rural woodland.

This is an enjoyable area for a short ramble, and a very convenient stopping point if waiting for a Heathrow arrival.

Facilities

At The Five Bells (0208 7594713), pub fare is served Mon-Sat, plus Sunday carvery. Well-behaved dogs on leads are welcome in the front bar and at the outside tables front and rear. Campervan access.

Getting there
From Junction 7 take the A4, Maidenhead. Enter Burnham village. At the roundabout take exit 1, B3026 Eaton, Lake End Road. Enter Dorney and pass a pub on the right. Drive over the river and the car park is on the left.

Return to M4 Junction 7
Turn right from the car park. At the roundabout take exit 3, signed A4 Slough. At the next roundabout take exit 3 signed M4 and return to the motorway.

The walk
Walk to the clearly-marked entrance to the Jubilee River Way. This is an all-access path along side the Jubilee 'River;' actually, a flood management device which has created 11km of wetlands.

Continue straight as far as the bridge where there's a choice of waymarked routes, as well as viewing platforms and information boards describing the wetlands. The public footpath running parallel to the main track divides walkers from cyclists. Turn around at a halfway point of your choice to return to the car park.

Facilities
Free car park, with height restrictions. There's a Sainsburys on the Lake End Road roundabout for picnic supplies.

Chieveley Services RG18 9XX

Getting there
Leave the M4 at Junction 13 and follow signs to Chieveley Services/
Costa. Park in the services car park as close as possible to the
Travelodge Motel.

Return to M4 Junction 13
Turn left from the services exit and rejoin the motorway.

The walk
This is a truly rural walk, and a surprising contrast to the busy
motorway and services nearby.

Walk past the Travelodge motel with the lorry and caravan parking
area on the right, and between the wooden posts in the corner onto a
lane. At the second footpath sign turn right to cross a stile into a field.

Continue straight, with the service road to your right. At a red sign
turn right and enter a field. Follow the yellow arrow to a lone tree some
distance away.

At the tree, bear half left and follow the narrow path towards
the trees ahead. Pass a group of three oak trees to reach a wooden
footbridge over a brook. This
brings you to a cart track, aptly
named Marsh Lane.

Turn right and walk as
far as the farm before turning
around. In hot weather, this
is a fantastic place to cool
overheated travelling dogs,
with plenty of drinking water
and splashing opportunities
provided by the brook. Retrace
your steps to return to the car
park.

Facilities
Moto motorway services
with Costa, M&S, Burger King.
Children's play area. Campervan
access.

Getting there

From Junction 15, take the A419 Swindon road, then first left, A4259 Swindon turn-off. At the roundabout take exit 1, A4259 Swindon. At the next roundabout take exit 1, signed Coate Water, to reach the car park down a lane on the left.

Return to M4 Junction 15

Leave the car park and take exit 5 at the roundabout, signed M4. Pass a Texaco petrol station on the left, and get in lane to return to the M4 at the next roundabout.

The walk

This is a fine, all-weather walk on a hard surface path around the lake.

From the car park, take the incline to the information board. The signed path around Coate Water is 4 miles of flat, easy walking. As this is a circular walk, it's easy to walk as far around the lake as you want, and turn around at a point that suits you.

Facilities

Free car park. WC. Café. Picnic area. BBQ area. Children's play area. Ranger on duty.

The Sun Inn (01793 523292) is adjacent to the lake, and a popular refreshment stop for families with children. Pub food is available from 1200. Dogs welcome in the large beer garden.

walking THE DOG

Lydiard Park SN5 3PA

Getting there

From Junction 16 take the A3102,
Swindon. At the roundabout take
exit 1, West Swindon, Lydiard Park.
At the next roundabout take exit 1, Lydiard Park and Hook. Turn right
signed Lydiard Park, then turn left into the car park.

Return to M4 Junction 16

Turn right from the car park and then left on to the main road. At the
roundabout take exit 3, M4, Wootton Bassett. At the next roundabout
take exit 3, M4.

The walk

Pass the visitor centre and café and turn right at a wooden post for the
circular Lakeside Walk. Continue straight ahead with the side of Lydiard
House to your left, and follow the rolling grassland gently downhill to
the lake. Cross the bridge on the left and then turn right into a wooded
area. Pass some picnic tables and follow the path round to return to the
green.

There's plenty of space to relax and ramble in this 260 acre park,
and a visit to the house and museum is an idea for non-walkers.

Facilities

Free car park closes at dusk. WC+RADAR. Café. Visitor centre.
Children's playground and exhibitions. Campervan access.

Lydiard House and Walled Gardens open Tues-Sun 1100-1600.
Entrance charges apply.

Getting there
From Junction 17 take the A429 Cirencester road. Turn left, signed Grittleton, Stanton St Quinton. Enter Stanton St Quinton and turn left, signed Kington St Michael, Kington Lane. Enter Kington St Michael, turn left at the T-junction and park at The Jolly Huntsman on the right. For non-patrons, there's more parking space opposite the village hall a little further on.

Return to M4 Junction 17
Turn right from the car park, then left at the crossroads. Turn left onto the A350. Continue on this road to rejoin the M4.

The walk
Turn left from the car park, walk past the Almshouses and turn right at a Public Bridleway sign.

When the path divides by a metal gate, take the right-hand path to walk through a meadow. In summer this is a mass of wildflowers, and the path is fringed with sweetly-scented chamomile.

Follow the clear path as far as the cottage on the left, and then turn around to return.

Facilities
At The Jolly Huntsman (01249 750305). Lunch 1200-1400. Well-behaved dogs on leads are welcome inside. Campervan access.

Caerleon NP18 1QQ

Getting there
From Junction 24 take the B4237, signed Newport. Turn right onto the B236 Caerleon, Royal Oak Hill. Turn right, signed The Bell Inn. Park on the right in The Bell Inn car park.

Return to M4 Junction 24
Turn left from the car park and left again up the hill. Continue to a T-junction and turn left, unsigned. This road leads directly to the M4.

The walk
Turn right from the car park and walk down the quiet lane beyond the pub for a few minutes until reaching a public footpath sign on the right, just after a house called Ty Bryn.

The path begins with steps up a steepish bank, a metal fence to your right. As the ground levels, the path opens out and, on a clear day, there's a magnificent view over the River Usk, and the town of Caerleon below.

Continue to follow the clear signs for the Usk Valley Way walk, with a blue and white otter symbol, and turn around at a point of your choosing to return to The Bell.

Facilities
The Bell (01633 420613) is a traditional inn open 1200-2300, and serving locally-sourced food. Well-behaved dogs on leads welcome in the front bar area. Campervan access.

Getting there

From Junction 27 take the B4591 signed High Cross; eastbound exit 1, westbound exit 3. Turn right – Cefn Walk – signed Fourteen Lock Canal Centre. The canal centre car park is on the right, just over a canal bridge.

Return to M4 Junction 27

Turn left out of the car park, drive over the canal bridge, and at the T-junction turn left. Follow this road to rejoin the motorway.

The walk

Walk away from the visitor centre to a gravel path leading downhill, passing top-up ponds for the canal system. When the path divides into steep and steeper, choose the steep option and walk through the vestiges of the fourteen locks,

where the engineering skills of the Victorians can't fail to impress.

The 'steeper' path follows the route of the canal through woodland and, if you don't mind the stiff climb back to the car park, is the longer of the two walks.

Facilities

Free car park, locked at dusk. WC. Visitor centre (01633 894 802). Campervan access. Small mini-market by the canal bridge has simple picnic fare.

walking THE DOG

Tredegar House NP10 8YW

Getting there
From Junction 28 take exit 4 eastbound, exit 2 westbound, signed Tredegar House. Follow the sliproad to the left, signed A48 and Tredegar House. At the lights turn left, and take exit 1 at the roundabout to enter the grounds of Tredegar House.

Return to M4 Junction 28
Leave the grounds and take exit 4 at the roundabout to join the A48 Newport road. At the traffic lights turn right, signed M4/A48 Newport, and follow the A48 to return to the motorway.

The walk
Go through the visitor centre entrance and continue to the front of Tredegar House to enter the 90 acre parkland and Woodland Trail. Dogs can run off-lead here.

This is an ideal walk if you're travelling with non-walkers as there's so much to see in and around the house, which was once home to the notorious Morgan family of pirates. The house has been a TV setting for *Dracula*, *Dr Who* and *Torchwood*.

Facilities
P&D car park. WC+disabled. Café. Craft shops. Free dog poo bags from the visitor centre. Campervan access.

Getting there

From the Junction 30 roundabout take the turning for Rudry. At a mini roundabout take exit 2, signed 'Through Traffic.' This is a narrow lane with passing places. Pass a farm on the right and then turn left at a T-junction, signed Lisvane. A Forestry Commission car park is on the right.

Return to M4 Junction 30

Turn left out of the car park and take the first right turn (unsigned). Cross the mini roundabout to rejoin the motorway.

The walk

Take the broad track leading gently uphill between the trees. In wet weather this track is the firmest path and provides a clear route to follow.

It's uphill for the first half and obviously downhill on the way back. Enticing trails lead off to left and right, and are worth exploring.

This is a dream spot for dog walkers, and a delightfully remote place to ramble in glorious solitude.

Facilities

Free parking at forest. Campervan access. Cardiff Gate motorway services are on the exit roundabout from the motorway.

M4
Junction
32

Castell Coch CF15 7JS

Getting there
From Junction 32 take the A4054, Tongwynglais. Enter Tongwynglais and turn right at The Lewis Arms, signed Castell Coch. Turn left at the Castell Coch tourist sign and drive up the hill to the car park.

Return to M4 Junction 32
Leave the castle grounds through the narrow gateway and turn right. Turn left at the T-junction and continue to rejoin the M4.

The walk
Before starting this walk, it's worth taking a (free) look at this fairytale castle from the path around the base. Castell Coch has been a location for *Doctor Who*, and was Cackle's Academy in *The Worst Witch* TV series.

    The walk starts from the top car park by the castle entrance. Take the clear path up the hill under the trees near an information board, and join the waymarked Taff Trail.

    The Trail runs from the castle to the town of Caerphilly, and offers the opportunity of a walk as long and as strenuous as you wish.

Facilities
Free car park 0930-1830. WC, café and shop inside the castle (entry charge). Only guide dogs allowed inside. Campervan access.

Getting there
From Junction 33 take the A4232 Cardiff, Penarth, Barry. Take the first slip road off the dual carriageway signed Museum of Welsh Life.

Return to M4 Junction 33
Exit the car park to the A4232 and return to the M4.

The walk
A museum may seem a strange place for a walk, but this is a 100 acre museum. As part of the experience the walk is outdoors, from where you can peep in at traditional Welsh dwellings, or shop at a working bakery with superb fresh bread and cakes for sale. There's also a school, farm, chapel, and craft workshops.

Dogs are welcome in the museum, and water bowls are plentiful.

There are safe places to attach dogs outside any exhibits that they aren't allowed into, such as the chapel.

Facilities
P&D car park, includes museum admission, 1000-1700. WC+disabled. Café. Shops. Exhibits. Hard surface paths. Campervan access. Free dog poo bags from reception.

Tyn-y-Coed Forest

Getting there

From Junction 34 take the A4119; eastbound exit 1, westbound exit 3. At the traffic lights turn right, signed Groes Faen. After Groes Faen turn right, Tynant Road. Enter Creigiau and turn left at the T-junction. Turn right, Tyn-y-Coed Road. A small Forestry Commission car park is on the left, shortly after a hospital driveway.

Return to M4 Junction 34

Turn right out of the car park. At the crossroads turn left. Pass a golf club and turn right, Tynant Road. At the T-junction turn right, Groes Faen, with the Dynevor Arms on the left. At the next T-junction turn left, signed M4.

The walk

Walk down the shingle track leading from the car park and through a kissing gate to enter the forest. A route is waymarked, although there is essentially just one surfaced, all-weather wheelchair/buggy-friendly path.

With no navigational skills necessary, this is a great place to inhale big lungfuls of healthy forest air.

Facilities

Free parking at Tyn-y-Coed. Campervan access. At The Dynevor Arms (0292 0890530, CF72 8NS) pub food is served 1200-1400; 1800-2100. Dogs on leads are welcome in the garden.

Getting there

Follow signs to Bryncethin. Enter Bryncethin, Bryncoch and turn left at a roundabout. At a T-junction turn left. At the next roundabout turn right, signed Abergwr, A4065. Enter Brynmenin and turn right, signed Bryngarw. Turn right, signed Bryngarw, to enter the grounds of Bryngarw House and the car park is on the right.

Return to M4 Junction 36

Leave the car park and grounds to turn left at the T-junction. Turn left again at the next T-junction and continue straight on the A4065 Bridgend. At the roundabout, take the 2nd exit, signed M4 and A4061 Bridgend. At the lights turn right, signed M4, and rejoin the motorway.

The walk

Walk past the house towards the plant nursery. Turn right at the unmarked public footpath just before the nursery gate. After a few paces there's a yellow waymark arrow. Follow these yellow markers and ignore all other trail signs.

Pass a pond on the right and continue to another yellow waymark. Go over a stile and into the ocean of bracken that follows. The path opens out to give a stunning vista of the valleys and ridge beyond. Follow the path into the woodland ahead, and retrace your route to return.

Facilities

At Bryngarw, free parking in term time. WC+disabled. Information room. Garden centre. Café/snacks available during school holidays. Campervan access. Sarn Park motorway services at the M4 exit.

walking THE DOG

Kenfig Dunes CF33 4PT

Getting there

From Junction 37 take the A4229, Porthcawl. At the next two roundabouts take the A4229 Porthcawl exits, then immediately turn right signed Kenfig. Pass a holiday park on the right, and turn right at a T-junction. Enter Kenfig and park in a small car park on the left by a nature centre.

Return to M4 Junction 37

Turn right out of the car park and then left after the golf clubhouse. Pass the holiday park and turn left at the T-junction, signed Port Talbot M4. At the roundabout take exit 1, M4 to return to the motorway.

The walk

The walk starts at the yellow waymark arrow behind the nature reserve building. Take a sandy track into the dunes to a green waymark arrow. Follow the green arrows for a circular sweep through the dunes. Look out for the rare Fen Orchid as you walk through carpets of wildflowers and exotic reed beds.

Kenfig has plenty of drama, from sunken villages to ghosts. It's an outstandingly attractive area, and has been featured in the TV series *Coast*.

Facilities

Free parking. WC and information at the nature centre; opening times vary. Campervan access.

The Prince of Wales pub (01656 740356) just beyond the car park is a popular local hostelry, where dogs are welcome in the bar.

Getting there
From Junction 40 take the A4107, Cymer. At the roundabout turn left, Cymer, Afon Argoed Forest. Continue for nearly 6 miles until the Afon Forest Park and visitor centre is signed to the right.

Return to M4 Junction 40
Turn left from the car park to the A4107, signed Port Talbot. At the mini roundabout turn right, signed M4 and Port Talbot, and rejoin the motorway.

The walk
Afon Forest is a vast,11,000 hectare centre for outdoor pursuits, including mountain biking, bird-watching, and hiking.

There are six marked trails of varying lengths, all starting at the visitor centre. This is unbeatable walking country and it's worth allowing plenty of time for extreme leg stretching.

Walkers and mountain bikes are kept apart by some very skilled route planning, so keep safely to the trails.

Facilities
Car park charges vary. WC.
Visitor centre. Café. Shop.
Campervan access.

Cwm Clydach

Getting there
From Junction 45 take the A4067(N), signed Pontadawe. At the roundabout take exit 1, B4291 Clydach. At a mini roundabout go straight across (B4603), and then take exit 2 at the next mini roundabout. Leave the town and continue. Pass The New Inn on the right, cross a bridge over a river and take an immediate right turn to enter the Cwm Clydach car park.

Return to M4 Junction 45
Turn left from the car park and continue. Take exit 1 at a mini roundabout, A4067 Swansea direction. At the next roundabout take exit 3, A4067 Swansea, M4.

The walk
Proceed through the metal gate to enter the nature reserve. There's just one path, which runs alongside the River Clydach, so the route is there-and-back. The path itself is exceptionally well maintained, and stays firm in wet weather.

Facilities
Free parking in nature reserve car park. Campervan access.
    The New Inn (01792 842839) does food but times vary. Children's play area. Dogs allowed in beer garden only.

Getting there
From Junction 46 follow signs to
Felindre. Enter Felindre. Turn right,
signed Ammanford, Rhydaman (this
turning is easy to miss). Take the 1st
right turn and park at The Shepherds
Country Inn.

Return to M4 Junction 46
Turn left from the car park and left at
the T-junction. Turn left at the next
T-junction, and continue to the M4.

The walk
Turn right to walk up a lane past a
trout fishery. Turn right at a green
footpath sign. Cross a stile with
waymark for the Gower Way.

Bear half right across a field and
over another stile. Turn left and walk
through an avenue of high bracken.
Cross two wooden footbridges to
follow the path along the side of a
valley. Climb the next two stiles and
continue as waymarked over a series
of wooden walkways above boggy
ground.

Rounding a corner, the outer wall of the Lliw reservoir is visible
ahead. Climb one final stile to reach a metalled lane at the corner of the
reservoir, then turn right to get to the visitor centre and café. Reverse
the route to return.

Facilities
Bar meals are served at the Shepherds Country Inn (01792 794715);
there's also a children's playground. Dogs on leads welcome in the bar
and beer garden. At the Lliw reservoir: WC. Outdoor café. Dog water.

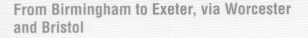
From Birmingham to Exeter, via Worcester and Bristol

Junction

Junction	
3	Woodgate Valley Country Park
4	Waseley Hills
5	Piper's Hill
7	Worcester Woods Country Park
11A	Crickley Hill
13	Frampton Green
17	Easter Compton
18	Blaise Castle Estate (northbound)
19	Leigh Woods
21	Sand Point
Sedgemoor Services	Brent Knoll (northbound)
22	Mark River Walk
23	Bawdrip, Somerset Levels
24	Maunsel Lower Lock
26	Buckland Wood
27	Sampford Peverell
31	Haldon Forest

Getting there

From Junction 3 take the A456, Kidderminster. Enter Halesowen and take the first left (unsigned), Lapal Lane South. Turn left just before a 'No through road' sign. At a crossroads turn right and then take exit 1 from the roundabout signed South Woodgate. The entrance to Woodgate Valley Country Park is on the left.

Return to M5 Junction 3

Turn right out of the park and return to the A456, then turn left. Continue to the roundabout at the bottom of the hill and double back to rejoin the motorway.

The walk

Three marked trails of between one and three miles have been created through the park, and maps are supplied at the visitor centre. Off-trail walking is encouraged within the 450 acres of the valley.

This is gentle, green rolling countryside, where it's hard to conceive that the heart of Birmingham is pumping not so very far away.

Facilities

Free parking 1000-1900 summer; til 1630 winter. WC. Refreshments. Visitor centre with outdoor seating. Picnic area. Children's play area. Campervan access.

Waseley Hills

Getting there

From Junction 4 take the A491, Stourbridge. Turn right signed Waseley Hills Country Park, B4551, Money Lane. Opposite a pub turn right, signed Waseley Hills Country Park. Turn right into the park and visitor centre.

Return to M5 Junction 4

Turn left from the park and continue to a T-junction. Turn left onto the B4551. At the junction with the A491, turn left to rejoin the M5.

The walk

There are two clearly-marked walks over the Waseley Hills. Both trails begin at the visitor centre and handy descriptive leaflets can be picked up before you start.

The Fox Trail (90 minutes) makes a circuit of the whole park, and is clearly signed with orange markers.

The shorter Badger Trail (30-40 minutes and purple markers) takes in magnificent views of the Black Country and Worcestershire on a bright day.

Facilities

P&D car park opens 0800 to dusk. WC+disabled. Visitor centre. Café. Children's play area. Campervan access.

Getting there

From Junction 5 follow signs to Bromsgrove, A38. Enter Wychbold and take the second right, Chequers Lane. At a T-junction turn left, Stoke Lane. Turn right, Astwood Lane. At the T-junction by The Country Girl turn right, Hanbury Road, and turn right to a car park just before a bend to the right.

Return to M5 Junction 5

Turn left from the car park. Turn left after The Country Girl. At the T-junction to Shore Lane turn left, Wychbold, and follow signs to return to the motorway.

The walk

Follow the path into the trees and downhill. Pass a large pond to the left and continue past Knotts Farm on the right to enter woodland.

Continue ahead on a clear path through glades of majestic trees. At a waymark post go straight on. Join a track, and follow the waymarked route. Continue into a field through a kissing gate.

Follow the clearly-marked footpath to the church and then retrace your steps through the wood and past Knotts Farm to return to the car park.

Facilities

Free car park. Campervan access. At The Country Girl (01527 821790; B60 4AY), open 1200-2300, lunch is served 1200-1430. Children welcome. Well-behaved dogs allowed in lounge.

walking THE DOG

Worcester Woods CountryPark WR5 2LG

Getting there

From Junction 7 take the A44, Worcester, Evesham. Continue on the A44 over two roundabouts and at the next roundabout take the A4440 Evesham exit. At the next roundabout take exit 1, signed Country Park, and enter Worcester Woods.

Return to M5 Junction 7

Leave the car park, take exit 3 at the roundabout, signed M5. Take exit 1 at the next roundabout and then rejoin the motorway.

The walk

Bear to the left of the visitor centre and proceed to a wooden sign for the Woodland Trail. Walk up the track and turn left at a waymark to the start of two, 30 minute, stile-free walks: a Woodland Trail, and a Meadows Trail.

Paths are well maintained and provide easy walking around this fully accessible route. Apparently, present-day Nunnery Wood was once cultivated by Cistercian nuns, who must have been pretty brawny to eke a living from this land.

Facilities

Free parking. WC+disabled. Visitor centre. Café. Picnic area. BBQ area. Shop. Children's playground. Campervan access.

Getting there

From Junction 11A follow signs to the A417, Cirencester. Crickley Hill Country Park is signed from the A417 Stow-on-the-Wold roundabout. The car parks are at the end of the entry lane.

Return to M5 Junction 11A

Leave the car park and turn right at the end of the lane. At the T-junction turn right, signed A417 Cirencester. Stay in the right-hand lane to take exit 2 A5/A417 signed Cheltenham Central, then follow signs to rejoin the M5.

The walk

There are marked routes for five walks of varying lengths, with descriptions and colour codes displayed on an information board. All walks begin at the visitor centre. At the start of the trails there's a viewpoint, with the Malvern Hills, Gloucester Cathedral, and the Black Mountains visible on a clear day.

The Family Trail (orange) is 0.5 miles, has no stiles, and is fairly buggy-friendly.

There are three 40 minute/0.75 mile walks: Hill Fort Trail, Scrubs Trail, and the Scarpe Trail. The Park Trail is slightly longer. All the trails are easy to follow, the main difference between them being the amount of shade in summer, or mud in wet weather.

Facilities

Free parking. WC. Visitor centre (April-Sept pm only). Picnic area. Free dog poo bags in car park. Dog water bowls.

Frampton Green GL2 7DY

Getting there
From Junction 13 take the A419/A38, Dursley. Turn right onto the
B4071, Frampton on Severn. Enter Frampton and turn left, signed
Frampton Green and churches. Look for The Three Horseshoes on the
right, and park nearby.

Return to M5 Junction 13
Return to the T-junction and turn right, signed Gloucester. At the
next T-junction turn left, A38 Gloucester/M5. At the roundabout take
exit 2, signed A419 Stroud/M5, and rejoin the motorway at the next
roundabout.

The walk
Cross the road from The Three Horseshoes to walk past Rosamunde
House and round a metal gate to the left of the sailing club entrance.
Take the left-hand path at the footpath sign ahead. Climb two stiles
(there's a dog gate on the second stile), and head across a field, aiming
for a brushwood arch. Climb a stile to the left of the arch and bear
half-left and through a gate ahead. Cross the lane after the next gate,
passing a house called Fitcherberry East, and proceed through another
gate. Aim for the weeping willows by the lake beyond. Turn at the lake
to return to the village green.

Facilities
The Three Horseshoes (01452 740463) is what village pubs are all
about! Food and snacks are available, and strangers are greeted with
lively interest. Well-behaved dogs on leads are welcome in the bar.
Campervan access.

East Compton BS35 5RA

Getting there
From Junction 17 take the B4055, Easter Compton. Continue to Easter Compton and park at The Fox Inn on the left.

Return to M5 Junction 17
Turn right from The Fox Inn car park and return to the motorway, B4055.

The walk
Cross the road from The Fox and turn left. Turn right at a white gate marked 'Collingwood,' and cross the stile ahead. Follow a footpath arrow over the first field, and climb a stile to enter field two. Walk across the field diagonally, with an electricity pole to your left.

Go through a gate to field three and follow the arrow into field four; walk diagonally to the far right-hand corner. Climb two stiles and enter field five. Walk along the left side of the field with the fence on the left. Turn around here to give a 40 minute walk.

Facilities
At The Fox Inn (01454 632220) food and snacks are served. Well-behaved dogs on leads are welcome in the bar. Campervan access.

walking THE DOG

Blaise Castle Estate   Northbound only

Getting there
Leave the M5 at Junction 18 to take the A4, signed Bristol, Docks. Remain on the A4 Bristol until a left turn – B4054 Shirehampton. Turn left, B4057, for the signed public car park on the right.

Return to M5 Junction 18
Turn left out of the car park. At the traffic lights turn right (Sylvan Way). Turn right at the next traffic lights, signed M5.
At the roundabout take exit 2 signed M5, and watch carefully for the lane changes.

The walk
This is an enormous outdoor space, with a mixture of woodlands, meadows, and limestone gorge spread over 650 acres.

Signed trails lead from the car park in all directions, to the point where you're spoiled for choice. Many paths are hard-surfaced for buggy and wheelchair accessibility.

The dog-friendliness of the estate is obvious as soon as you walk towards the café, to be greeted by a large contemporary dog sculpture, with built-in water bowl.

On sunny days this is a popular destination, and you may find queues for the café and car park.

Facilities
Free car park. WC+disabled. Café. Children's play area. Campervan access.

Getting there
From Junction 19 take the A369, Easton in Gordano. Proceed on the A369. Pass The George in Abbots Leigh and turn left at the slightly obscured sign to Leigh Woods. Continue up a long driveway to reach the car park on the left.

Return to M5 Junction 19
Turn right out of the entrance lane, A369, and continue to return the M5.

The walk
This is a fabulous walk through Forestry Commission woods with clear paths and easy-to-follow routes.

Two marked trails begin from the car park. The red route is two miles; the purple route is a little shorter at 1.5 miles, and passes by the site of an iron-age hill fort.

It's also easy to ramble on your own route underneath the canopy of trees. When we were here the birdsong was awesome and the wood was as close to deserted as anyone could wish for.

Facilities
Free parking. Campervan access.

Sand Point

Getting there
From Junction 21 take the A370, Weston-super-Mare. Take the first exit off the A370, signed B3440 Kewstoke. At the traffic lights turn right, Kewstoke. Pass a McDonalds on the left and follow signs to Kewstoke across several small roundabouts. Enter Kewstoke and continue straight on. Turn right signed Sand Bay. Turn right at the T-junction 'Sand Point Only,' and park at the end of the lane.

Return to M5 Junction 21
Turn left out of the car park, and left again into Sand Road, signed Bristol. At the T-junction turn left, signed Worle. Continue over the next three roundabouts. Get into the left-hand lane before the T-junction, and follow signs to rejoin the M5.

The walk
Enter the Middle Hope Nature reserve on the surfaced path to the right of the information board. The circular path is easy to follow, and keen eyes may spot the site of a motte and bailey castle – the remains of Thomas a Beckett's Priory – and even a Neolithic barrow.

Dog walkers may prefer the beach walk. The beach is large, and a path runs parallel to the lane which stretches for miles.

Facilities
Free parking. WC. Campervan access. National Trust dog toilet area. Tearoom with home-baked cakes on Sand Road.

Getting there

Sedgemoor Services are between M5 Junctions 22 and 21 on the northbound side of the motorway. No southbound access.

Return to M5 northbound

As signed from Sedgemoor Services.

The walk

Park on the left side of the car park. Walk past a 'No Entry' sign to a service road and over a cattle grid. Turn left and pass Strowland Cottage. Turn right at a footpath sign and follow a yellow pointer across a field, and then go over a wooden footbridge and stile hidden in the hedge. Brent Knoll is on the left.

Walk with the hedge to your right and the Knoll ahead. Keep a pylon on your left and cross a footbridge into the third field. Turn around here for a 30 minute walk.

Brent Knoll was once an island. Folklore says it was created from a wayward shovelful of soil thrown here by the same giant who dug out Cheddar Gorge.

Facilities

Welcome Break motorway services. Coffee Primo. Eat-in. Burger King. Children's playground. Days Inn motel (dog-friendly). Campervan access.

Mark River Walk TA9 4LT

Getting there

From Junction 22 take exit 1, A38, Highbridge. Take the first left, B3139 Mark. At a T-junction turn left, B3139 Mark. Enter Mark, and park at The White Horse Inn on the left.

Return to M5 Junction 22

Turn right from the car park and follow the lane back through Mark. Turn right signed A38/M5 Edith Meade. Turn right at the T-junction, A38 Bristol. At the roundabout take exit 3 and rejoin the motorway.

The walk

Take a left from the car park, passing in front of The White Horse. Continue past some cottages with Vole Road to the left to a Public Bridleway.

This becomes a grassy track with water flowing on the right. The path is some 2.5m wide with plenty of dog romping space and an abundance of wildlife.

Follow the waterway as far as you wish before turning around to return to The White Horse.

Facilities

At the White Horse Inn (01278 641234), lunch is available from midday. Beer garden, children's play area. Dogs welcome in the bar and beer garden. Campervan access.

Getting there

From Junction 23 take the A39, Glastonbury/Wells. At a T-junction turn left, A39 Glastonbury. After 300 yards turn left into The Knowle Inn car park.

Return to M5 Junction 23

Turn left from the car park and then right onto the A39 to return to the motorway.

The walk

Cross the road in front of the pub and turn right. Immediately turn left at a footpath sign. This soon becomes a secluded path between two high hedges. After the left side hedge ends, climb a stile on the right to walk across the field and over the next stile.

Follow the yellow arrow to the left in field two. Walk with the hedge to your left around the corner of the field to a gate on the left. Cross the next stile by the gate and continue to a footbridge, and one more stile.

Cross King Sedgmoor's Drain bridge and turn right after the kissing gate to walk with the water on your right. For a 35 minute walk, turn around here.

The walk can be extended by continuing along the waterside.

Facilities

At the 16th century Knowle Inn (01278 683330) quality meals and snacks are served all day, plus cream teas. Well-behaved dogs on leads are welcome in the large beer garden and public bar. Campervan access.

Maunsel Lower Lock

Getting there
From Junction 24 take the A38, Bridgwater, Minehead. At the next
roundabout take exit 1, Taunton A38. Enter North Petherton and turn
left after a church, signed North Newton. At North Newton turn left
(Maunsel Road), and follow the small tourist signs for 'Canalside Walk.'
Eventually turn left, signed Canal
Centre/Bankland. The car park is on
the left before the canal bridge.

Return to M5 Junction 24
Turn right from the car park. At the
T-junction turn right and follow the
brown signs to Maunsel House.
Enter North Newton. Continue to
a T-junction and turn right, signed
Bridgwater. At the next T-junction
turn right, A38 Bridgwater. At a
small roundabout take exit 3 to
return to the M5.

The walk
Cross the canal bridge and walk down to the canal. The towing path to
the right is hard surfaced, wide, and suitable for all weathers and shoes.
The path in the opposite direction is unsurfaced, muddier, and more
popular with dog walkers.

Facilities
Free parking. WC. Tea Rooms
(Wed-Sun 1030-1700). Bridgwater
Moto motorway services at the M5
exit roundabout with Burgerking,
Fresh Express. Campervan access.

Buckland Wood EX15 3TR

Getting there

From Junction 26 take the Blackmore/Ruggin turn. At a T-junction turn right, signed Ford Street. Bear right as the road forks, and at a T-junction turn left, signed Ford Street. Continue through Ford Street, ignoring all side turnings. At the top of the hill turn left, signed Kingsmeade Centre, and continue to park at The Merry Harriers on the right.

Return to M5 Junction 26

Turn left from the car park. At the crossroads turn right, signed Wellington. Continue through Ford Street and then turn right, signed Blackmore. At the next signpost turn left, signed Wellington, to return to the M5.

The walk

Cross the road and bear right. Turn left at a Public Bridleway sign on the left. Go through a gate, and follow the arrow straight ahead: there is a splendid view over the countryside below from this point. Follow the track downhill through the trees, then turn around and return uphill to The Merry Harriers.

Facilities

The Merry Harriers (01823 421270) is a gastro pub with award-winning food. Open Tuesday 1200 to Sunday afternoon. Well-behaved, clean dogs are permitted in the bar and large outdoor area. Campervan access.

walking THE DOG

Sampford Peverell EX16 7BJ

Getting there

From Junction 27 take the A361, Barnstaple/Tiverton. Take the 1st slip road, left, and at a mini roundabout turn left, signed Sampford Peverell. Enter Sampford Peverell and park at The Globe Inn on the right.

Return to M5 Junction 27

Turn left from the car park, continue to the roundabout and take exit 3. Rejoin the M5 at the next roundabout.

The walk

Walk to the rear of the overspill car park and up the small flight of steps leading straight onto the towing path of the Grand Western Canal.

This canal was intended to link the Bristol and English Channels, but that 19th century grand design was never completed, and now the 11 miles or so of canal have become the Great Western Canal country park.

Look out for horse-drawn barges hauling their cargo of 21st century tourists along the waterway.

Facilities

The timbered Globe Inn (01884 821214) has all-day opening and food. Children's playground with lots of activities. Dogs welcome in the public bar and outside. Campervan parking on-road if the entry archway to the car park is a challenge.

Getting there

Leave the M5 and follow the A380, Torquay. After a long bend to the right, turn left signed Great Howelden. Pass a café and turn left at a Give Way sign. Turn right, signed Ashcombe/Dawlish. At a crossroads go straight, signed Ashcombe. Turn left into the Mamhead Forest car park.

Return to M5 Junction 31

Turn right from the car park. At the crossroads turn left, signed Chudleigh/Newton Abbot. At the dual carriageway turn left – A380 Torquay. Turn onto the B3192, Teignmouth road. At the roundabout take exit 3 signed Exeter M5. Pass a Texaco garage on the left, merge with the A38 and continue, following signs to the M5.

The walk

There is a circular trail around Haldon Forest that starts at the information board in the car park. The path is fully accessible and marked with a blue shoeprint symbol. On a clear day you can see Exmouth, the Black Forest, and the Jurassic coastline.

An ideal spot for a picnic and some quiet time at the furthest point of the M5.

Facilities

P&D parking. Picnic area. Campervan access.

From Rugby to Carlisle, via Birmingham and Preston

Junction

Junction	
1	Swift Valley Nature Reserve
2	Oxford Canal
3	Hawkesbury Junction
7	Sutton Park
12	Shoal Hill
13	Acton Trussell
14	Worston
15	Hanchurch Hills
16	Barthomley Fields
18	Brereton Heath
20	Spud Wood
22	Culcheth Linear Park
23	Pennington Flash
26	Beacon Country Park
28	Cuerden Valley Park
33	Scorton Nature Trail
34	Crook o'Lune
38	Tebay Village
40	Pooley Bridge, Ullswater
42	Wetheral
44	Hadrian's Wall

Getting there

From Junction 1 take the A426, Rugby; northbound exit 1, southbound exit 3. At the roundabout take exit 2, Rugby A426. At the next roundabout take exit 3, Brownsover Hall. The entrance to the nature reserve car park is on the right after the Brownsover Hall Hotel.

Return to M6 Junction 1

Leave the car park and turn immediately right at the top of the slope, and then left onto the main road, signed M6, M1. Follow signs at three successive roundabouts to return to the motorway.

The walk

Follow the path slightly uphill from the car park to reach a canal bridge, and go through a gate into the field beyond.

Walk across the lower part of the field to the next gate, which leads onto a tranquil towpath by a disused canal that's now a haven for wildlife.

At a blue footpath sign turn away from the towpath into wilder, woodland territory. The path is clearly signed and returns directly to the car park.

Facilities

Free parking, 1.8m height restriction. Non-residents welcome at the adjacent Brownsover Hall Hotel (01788 546100). Dogs may accompany owners to the elegant outside seating area.

Oxford Canal CV7 9HZ

Getting there
From Junction 2 take the
B4065, signed Ansty. Enter
Ansty and park at The Rose
and Castle Inn on the right.

Return to M6 Junction 2
Turn left from the car park, and
return to the M6 on the B4065.

The walk
This 77 mile long canal links
Oxford with Coventry. Unlike
other industrial canal routes,
the Oxford canal never became
a 19th century cargo super-
highway, and so today it one
of the most enjoyable rural
towpath walks in the country.

From the rear of the car
park walk down to the canal.
Cross the bridge and go
through a gate on the right to
reach the towpath. Turn right
and walk under the bridge.

A walk to Bridge 19 and
back is a 30 minute stroll, with
the option of a longer walk by
simply continuing along the
towpath.

Facilities
At the Rose and Castle (024 7661 2822) food is served from midday,
Mon-Sat. Dogs allowed in rear outdoor seating area. Campervan
access.

Getting there

From Junction 3 take the B4113, Bedworth. At the next roundabout take exit 2, Bedworth, B4113. At the traffic lights turn right – Black Horse Road. At a mini roundabout take exit 2. Cross a canal bridge and turn left to park by The Greyhound.

Return to M6 Junction 3

Leave The Greyhound and turn right. Continue on Black Horse Road to a T-junction. Turn left, B4113. At the roundabout take exit 3, signed M6, and return to the motorway.

The walk

The Canal Art Trail towpath walk between Hawkesbury Junction and the Coventry Basin is interesting and different, as it features artworks commissioned from local artists.

Look out for the imposing statue of the famous 18th century canal engineer James Brindley in particular.

The path is well-maintained and buggy-friendly. The complete Art Trail is 5 miles, and leads into the City of Coventry.

Facilities

At the Greyhound Inn (02476 363046), well-behaved dogs are welcome in the bar area here, and children are allowed inside until 1900. Campervan access.

Sutton Park B74 2YT

Getting there
From Junction 7 take the A34, Birmingham. At the second set of traffic lights turn left, Queslett Road. At a roundabout go straight across – Brownhills A4041. At the next roundabout turn right, King's Road. At the next roundabout take exit 3, Rough Road. Continue and take a left turn signed Tamworth A453. Pass a leisure centre and turn left to enter Sutton Park.

Return to M6 Junction 7
Leave through the Town Gate and turn right. At the traffic lights turn right, Monmouth Drive. Go straight at the lights and take exit 3 at the roundabout, King's Road. At the next roundabout turn left. Continue straight at the next roundabout and turn right at the lights, A34, to return to the M6.

The walk
Sutton Park is the largest urban park in Europe with 2400 acres of open space containing seven lakes and a mixed terrain of heathland, woodland, wetlands, and marshes. Pause at the visitor centre to pick up a leaflet of the eight varied walk routes here. Archaeological walk routes trace a Roman road, and pass evidence of prehistoric Brummies. You may see wild cattle and ponies, or even a stoat.

Facilities
P&D car parks 0900 to dusk. WC+disabled. Visitor centre. Café, bistro, steakhouse within the park. Rangers on duty throughout the park. Campervan access.

Getting there
Leave the M6 at Junction 12 and take the A5, Cannock. Turn left, Huntington, opposite the Four Crosses pub. At a crossroads, go straight, signed Huntington, Cocksparrow Lane. Shoal Hill car park is the first turning on the right.

Return to M6 Junction 12
Turn left from the car park. At the crossroads go straight across. Continue and turn right onto the A5 to return to the M6.

The walk
This is a magnificent walk over the lower reach of Cannock Chase. The land is laced with paths, and the open heathland makes it easy to navigate. There are no signed trails.

The paths leading away from the car park incline gently upward, and so the return to the car park is an easy, downhill stroll.

Facilities
Free car park (closes dusk), with height restriction. At the 17th century Four Crosses Inn (01543 503309, WS11 1RX) dogs on leads are allowed in the bar.

Acton Trussell ST17 0RJ

Getting there
From Junction 13 take the A449, Stafford. At a roundabout take exit 3 signed Acton Trussell (Mill Lane). Enter Acton Trussell and continue to the Moat House and car park at the far end of the village.

Return to M6 Junction 13
Turn left out of the car park and continue through the village. Turn left at the roundabout, exit for A449 Wolverhampton and M6, and rejoin the motorway.

The walk
Walk past the entrance to the Moat House. Go through a gate and turn left, then left again following a yellow footpath sign over the canal bridge.

Turn left onto the towing path of the Staffordshire and Worcestershire canal, and enjoy a flat but interesting walk past brightly-painted narrowboats and calm Staffordshire countryside.

The path is well maintained and delightfully rural.

Facilities
At the 14th century Moat House (01785 712217) food is available from 1200. Dogs are welcome at the outdoor tables by the side of the lake. Campervan access.

Getting there
From Junction 14 take the A5013, Eccleshall. Pass through Creswell and Gt Bridgford, and turn right at a tourist sign for The Mill at Worston, Worston Lane. Park at The Mill on the left.

Return to M6 Junction 14
Turn right from the car park. At the T-junction turn left, and continue to return to the M6.

The walk
After parking return to the road and turn right past a livery stable. Cross to a footpath sign and follow a yellow marker down a track. Follow the track on the left into a field and walk through to the next yellow waymark, then over a stile, with dog hole. Cross a brook to enter the next field and follow the track straight ahead. Turn around at the gate at the end of this field to return the same way.

Facilities
At The Mill (01785 282710) food is available from 1200. Children's play area, easy wheelchair access. Dogs on leads in garden only. Campervan access.

walking THE DOG

Hanchurch Hills

Getting there
From Junction 15 take the A519, Eccleshall, Shrewsbury. Enter Hanchurch. At the traffic lights continue on the A519 and turn right, signed Stableford. Continue until the start of woodland, and turn left to the car parks.

Return to M6 Junction 15
Turn right out of the car park, and then left at the end of the lane to the A519. Stay on the A519 to rejoin the M6.

The walk
There are several clearly-marked trails in these wonderful woods, and the trail markers start from the second car park.

The Red route is about 2 miles (40 minutes), and the Green trail is just over 3 miles (90 minutes). If you have the time, there's a Blue trail at 7 miles.

The woodland here is perfect for children and dogs to really let off steam. Even on the hottest of days, the cooling canopy of branches provides shade.

Facilities
Free car park. Picnic tables. Campervan access.

Getting there

From Junction 16 take the B5078, Alsager. Turn left, signed Barthomley, and park by the White Lion Inn in the village.

Return to M6 Junction 16

Leave the village and turn right at a T-junction onto the B5078 to return to the M6.

The walk

From the White Lion walk to the church and turn left at a footpath sign. Pass the rectory and continue with a hedge to your right. Climb a stile with dog gate, bear left and over the next stile to enter a large field. Walk with the hedgerow to the left and cross the field with a dewpond to your left.

At the hedge at the far side, turn right and hunt for the almost invisible stile in the far corner. Carry straight across the next field, aiming for a metal gate and stile near the trees. Follow the arrow over the stile to a gate and waymark. Turn around here for a 40 minute walk.

Facilities

The White Lion Inn (01270 882242) is a 16th century inn that seems to be the second home of the entire village. Food served. Dogs on leads are welcome inside.

Brereton Heath

Getting there
From Junction 18 take the A54, Holmes Chapel. Enter Holmes Chapel and continue, signed Congleton. Turn right, Davenport Lane; the entrance to Brereton Heath Nature Reserve is on the left.

Return to M6 Junction 18
Turn right out of the car park. Turn left onto the A54 and continue to rejoin the motorway.

The walk
There are a number of trails in this 50 acre nature reserve, including an easy access trail around the perimeter of the lake.

Trail leaflets can be picked up from the information centre, and rangers are on hand to give advice.

Dog owners are encouraged to explore the woodland trails surrounding the lake, which is a popular dog swimming venue.

Facilities
P&D car park open 0830 to dusk. Visitor centre. WC+disabled. Picnic tables. Campervan access.

Getting there

From Junction 20 follow signs to join the B5158, Lymm. Enter Lymm and turn right, signed A56, Altrincham. At a roundabout turn left, Oughtrington Lane exit. Turn right after a canal bridge, Stage Lane. Spud Wood car park is on the right (unsigned).

Return to M6 Junction 20

Turn left out of the car park and then left onto Oughtrington Crescent. At the T-junction turn right, Higher Lane, then left onto Elm Tree Road. Continue to the M6.

The walk

This is a fabulous walking spot, with several good walks. A canal walk gives the choice of a 1.5 mile trail to the pretty town of Lymm, or a 2.5 mile walk to Dunham Park in the other direction.

The Timberland Trail starts at the car park. Cross the canal bridge and follow the signed path into Spud Wood, maintained by the Woodland Trust.

A wheelchair-accessible path (flat with a light gravel surface) is marked.

Facilities

Free parking. Campervan access. Shops and cafés in nearby Lymm, and a petrol station on the way with WCs and a small shop.

walking THE DOG

Culcheth Linear Park WA3 4AB

Getting there
From Junction 22 take exit 1 southbound; exit 3 northbound, Winwick Lane. Turn right at a sign to Croft, Sandy Brow Lane. At a T-junction in Croft turn left, Mustard Lane. The entrance to Culcheth Linear Park is a sharp turn to the left after a bridge.

Return to M6 Junction 22
Turn right out of the car park. Turn right after the school in Croft, signed Lowton. Turn left at the T-junction to return to the M6.

The walk
The park is linear because it used to be a railway line to Wigan. Now, though, it's a dreamy countryside environment in the Mersey Forest with hardly anyone around except walkers.

The park is about 2 miles long, with a circular route for a 45 minute walk. Free walks leaflets are available at the ranger cabin. The main path is hard surfaced and suitable for wheelchair users and buggies.

Facilities
Free parking. Picnic tables. Ranger cabin. Campervan access.

The Cherry Tree, Culcheth (01925 762624; WA3 4EX) is a modern pub serving food from 1200. Dogs welcome in the outdoor seating areas.

Getting there

From Junction 23 take the A580, Manchester. Turn left, signed Pennington Flash, A579, Bolton. Then turn left at traffic lights and right into Pennington Flash when signed, opposite a fire station.

Return to M6 Junction 23

Turn left out of the park and turn right at the traffic lights signed M6/Manchester A579. At the next traffic lights turn right, signed M6/A580, and continue to return to the M6.

The walk

There's plenty of space here for a good long walk, either on the signed trails or just rambling around the park's 200 hectares.

The main feature is the huge lake or 'flash,' which is home to a host of wildfowl, including black swans.

To reach the trails, pass the children's play area, and then there's a choice of a water path by the lake or a woodland path. The paths are well maintained and fully accessible, though shared with cyclists and horses.

Facilities

P&D car park. WC+disabled. Information centre. Mobile café. Children's play area. Dog water bowls. Campervan access.

Beacon Country Park WN8 7RU

Getting there
From Junction 26 follow signs to reach the A577, Wigan, and continue for 2 miles. Turn right onto Mill Lane and continue to Beacon Country Park. There are two car parks; the second is nearer to the visitor centre and facilities.

Return to M6 Junction 26
Turn right from either car park, then left onto the A577 and follow signs to return to the M6.

The walk
There are well-signed paths leading out from both car parks. The terrain

is a mixture of woodland and open grassland, with enough space for a good 45 minute walk or longer.

To reach the facilities at the visitor centre, leave either car park and follow the direction indicated on the trails. Wheelchair users can join an accessible circular track from the visitor centre, or from the second car park.

Facilities
Free parking. WC+disabled. Visitor centre. Café. Dog water. Ranger office. Campervan access.

Getting there

Leave the M6 at Junction 28 and turn right, signed A49, Euxton. Follow the brown signs to Cuerden Valley Park, going straight on at the traffic lights on Lancaster Lane. Go straight on at a mini roundabout, leave the residential area, and the Wigan Road car park is signed on the left.

Return to M6 Junction 28

Leave the Wigan Road car park and turn right. At the mini roundabout continue straight and rejoin the M6 as signed.

The walk

With 650 acres there's plenty of good walking at Cuerden Valley Park, and the marked paths are just a starting point.

Take the gravel, multi-access path from the car park and continue to a signed footpath to the lake. Turn right on the other side of the lake and follow the path through Dog Kennel Wood and Gravel Hole Wood. Turn right onto the multi-user path and then left, signed visitor centre. Walk past the front of Cuerden Hall to the Cinder Path. Turn left on the multi-user path to return to the car park.

Facilities

P&D car parks (6ft 6 height restriction). WC+disabled. Visitor centre, vending machine drinks. Picnic supplies available at Sainsbury's, off the A6/A49 junction.

Scorton Nature Trail PR3 1BY

Getting there
From Junction 33
take the A6, Garstang,
Blackpool. Turn left
at the staggered
junction, Whinney
Brow Lane. At a
T-junction turn right,
and then left over a
railway. Turn right,
Richmond Hill Lane.
At JC Country Shop
turn left, Clevely Park
Lane. Turn left at
the sign for Scorton
Picnic Site car park.

Return to M6 Junction 33
Turn right from the car park, and then right
at Miller's Brow. Turn left, Richmond Hill
Lane. Turn left and then right after the railway
bridge. Turn left, Whinney Brow Lane. Turn
right at the A6 junction. Take exit 2 at the
roundabout to rejoin the M6.

The walk
This is a hugely enjoyable, 30-40 minute, circular woodland walk with
one well-signed path, making navigation easy.

   Begin from the rear left corner of the car park on a well-maintained
track. Continue, following the circular walk route marked with white
arrows.

   A shallow river on the left at the start of the walk is ideal for cooling
down journey-fatigued dogs.

Facilities
Picnic tables at the start of the walk. JC Country Shop and Café (01524
791362). WC+disabled. Café. Farm shop. Outdoor clothing and pet
supplies. Campervan access.

Getting there

From Junction 34 take the A683, Kirkby Lonsdale. Turn left, Dennydeck Lane (unsigned) just before a group of cottages. Cross the 6ft wide bridge and turn right at a crossroads – Low Road. Turn left at a tourist sign to Crook O'Lune picnic site. Parking for wider vehicles and wheelchair users is just before the narrow bridge.

Return to M6 Junction 34

Turn right from the car park and turn left, Station Road, just before The Greyhound Inn. Breathe in and recross the narrow bridge. Turn right at the T-junction to return to the M6.

The walk

Paths within the Lune Millennium Park roughly follow the River Lune from Glasson to Lancaster, and Bull Beck near Caton. Start at Station 6 car park and go downhill on the single path to the river valley below. It's a 45 minute, 2km walk to Bull Beck, where there's a picnic area and WC.

The riverside path, starting at the alternative car park before the narrow bridge, is gradient-free and hard-surfaced. Pass the old station to join the Bull Beck path.

Facilities

Station 6: free parking til dusk. WC+RADAR. Café. Walk info. At Bull Beck: WC+disabled. Picnic tables. Campervan access.

Tebay Village CA10 3UY

Getting there
From Junction 38 take the A685, Kendal. Park at The Cross Keys Inn on the right, or along the lane by the churchyard.

Return to M6 Junction 38
Turn left from the car park and, at the roundabout, take exit 1 to rejoin the motorway.

The walk
Turn left out of the car park and left again; this is Church Street. Walk downhill with the churchyard to your left to find a yellow waymark arrow, then follow more yellow arrows leading around a barn.

Turn left onto a track and go straight on at a bridleway sign. Cross the river bridge ahead.

Turn right at a footpath sign to walk with the river on the right, and pass underneath the motorway. Continue along the path and over two stiles into a large field.

Towards the end of this field the remains of a motte and bailey castle can be reached by stepping stones. The river is broad, clean, and shallow here.

For a 40 minute walk, this is a good place to turn around.

Facilities
At the Cross Keys (0153 9624240) dogs are welcome in the bar. Campervan access.

Getting there

From Junction 40 take the A66, Keswick. At a roundabout take exit 2, A592, Ullswater. Turn left, B5320, Pooley Bridge. Park in the Dunmallard car park before the bridge.

Return to M6 Junction 40

Turn right from the car park. Turn right when A592 M6/Penrith signed. At the roundabout take exit 2 to return to the motorway.

The walk

The walk begins at the rear of the car park, where the path is very clear. Walk through the woodland with the clean and shallow River Eamont to your right, and eventually emerge into a field. Continue along the river bank for just under a mile, then turn around to return to the car park.

Facilities

P&D parking. Blue Badge holders free. Campervan access. At the timbered Pooley Bridge Inn (017684 86215) home-cooked food is served 1200-2030. Well-behaved dogs welcome throughout.

Wetheral CA4 8ES

Getting there
From Junction 42 take the B6263, Wetheral. Drive through Cumwhinton and enter Wetheral. Pass the village green on the right, and turn right by the General Stores. Park at The Crown Hotel on the left; non-patrons in the lane.

Return to M6 Junction 42
Turn left at the T-junction by the General Stores. Continue on this road to return to the M6.

The walk
There's a lot to admire on this walk, which combines a fabulous riverscape and fine walking with samples of glorious architectural bling.

Walk downhill from the hotel, past the station, and down a flight of 99 steps. Turn right onto a lane, past a church, and then turn left to reach the River Eden.

Don't miss the stone bench with faux-Victorian cushioned seats here, created by sculptor Tom Shutter.

Turn right and continue on the riverside path until a point opposite

a waterfall on the other side of the river. Climb the steps into Wetheral Woods, a slumbering ancient wood. After enjoying the wood for a while, turn around to return.

If you want to avoid climbing the 99 steps, take the grassy slope to cut through the churchyard, turn right on the lane, and then right by the General Stores.

Facilities
At Walton's Bar in the Crown Hotel (01228 561888) there's a good selection of meals and snacks from 1200. Well-behaved dogs on leads are welcome in the large bar area. Campervan access.

Getting there
From Junction 44 (and A74) take the A689, Hexham, and exit 1 at the next roundabout, A689. Turn right, signed Low Crosby. Enter Low Crosby and park in The Stag Inn car park.

Return to M6 Junction 44
Turn right out of the car park and right at the T-junction – Carlisle A689. At the roundabout take exit 3 signed M6/Scotland.

The walk
This is a flat, green and lovely walk along the river to Linstock and back. From the car park, turn right onto the road and follow the signed footpath for the Hadrian's Wall path. Walk to the end of the short lane and turn left, ignoring the first footpath sign and stile.

Turn right to walk with the River Eden on your left in the direction of Linstock on the Hadrian's Wall path, which is full of atmosphere and a sense of history, even though none of the wall remains.

Facilities
At the Stag Inn (01228 573210) food is served from 1200. Dogs are welcome in the lounge and beer garden. Campervan access.

From London to Cambridge, via Harlow

Junction

Getting there
From Junction 7 take the B1393, Epping. Pass a McDonalds on the left. Enter Thornwood Common and turn right, signed Epping Green, Uplands Road. Park in The Travellers Friend car park.

Return to M11 Junction 7
Turn right from The Travellers Friend. At the crossroads, turn left, B1393. Continue on this road to return to the M11.

The walk
Leave the car park and turn right down a broad, grassy track – Epping Long Green. The path along this linear village green is 2.5km in total. Early one Sunday morning in spring, this track was sparkling with dewy May bloom and buttercups, not a trace of the 21st century to be seen or heard. A delight for dogs and drivers.

Facilities
At The Travellers Friend (01992 572462), open 1200-2300, well-behaved dogs are welcome in the bar. Campervan access.

Hatfield Forest

Getting there

From Junction 8 take the B1256, Takeley. Enter Takeley and turn right opposite The Green Man, signed Hatfield Forest. Turn right where signed to enter the forest and car parks.

Return to M11 Junction 8

Turn left at the forest exit, and left again onto the B1256 to return to the M11 interchange.

The walk

There are a number of planned trails – including a discovery trail for children – within this enormous forest, and a leaflet of routes can be purchased from the NT kiosk on entry.

If you're here for just a short stroll, it's easy to find a convenient pathway from your starting point for a ramble through the trees.

Dogs that may chase wildlife must be kept on leads; other dogs off-lead except by the lake.

Facilities

National Trust car park charge, NT members free. WC+disabled. Café. Shop. All-terrain pushchairs available to loan. Campervan access. Birchhanger Green Services (Welcome Break) at the M11 exit.

Getting there

From Junction 10 take the A505, Royston. Turn right, signed Thriplow, Gravel Pit Lane. At a crossroads turn left, Farm Lane. Bear right onto Lower Street, and the Green Man (painted blue!) is on the left.

Return to M11 Junction 10

Turn right from The Green Man car park and bear left, Farm Lane. Turn right at the crossroads, and then turn left at the A505 to rejoin the motorway at the next roundabout.

The walk

Turn right from The Green Man and then left at a footpath sign by Yew Tree Cottage. At the end, turn left onto a lane, and immediately right at the next footpath sign. Follow the footpath signs to walk across fields to Church Lane. Turn right at a metal swing gate and pass Bacon's Farm. Turn left at a Bridleway sign. Walk for 20 minutes or so along this broad track, passing an RSPB information board describing the birds found in this area, and then retrace the route to the Green Man.

Facilities

The Green Man (01763 208855) serves light lunches and specials, using fresh local produce. Well-behaved dogs on leads are welcome in the rear garden. Campervan access.

Grantchester Meadows CB3 9NF

Getting there

From Junction 12 take the A603 Cambridge exit at the roundabout, then merge onto the Grantchester road. At the T-junction turn right, Coton Road, enter Grantchester and then turn left to reach The Red Lion car park. There's additional parking at the village charity car park on the right at the end of the village, a huge field, close to Byron's Pool.

Return to M11 Junction 12

Turn right onto High Street, then left, Coton Road. At the roundabout take exit 1, A603, and continue to return to the M11.

The walk

Turn right from the car park to enter Grantchester Meadows. There are two paths here: the higher path is hard-surfaced and used by buggies, bikes and wheelchairs; the lower path hugs the river, and has many access points to the water for dog-swimming. Both paths are easy to follow, and can be combined to form a 40 minute circular route.

Facilities

At The Red Lion (01223 840121) food is served 1100-2200. Children's play area. ATM machine. Dogs on leads welcome at outside tables. Campervan access.

Village charity car park – donations in honesty box.

M18

From Rotherham to Goole, via Doncaster

Junction

1	Roche Abbey
4	Sandall Beat Woods
6	Waterside

Roche Abbey

Getting there
From Junction 1 take the A631 towards Maltby, following tourist signs
to Roche Abbey. Turn right where signed, down a steep, cobbled,
private road with parking for Abbey visitors at the bottom.

Return to M18 Junction 1
Ascend the cobbled track, turn left. At the T-junction, turn left onto the
A631 and return to the M18.

The walk
This is a circular walk around the perimeter of the abbey ruins. Walk
through the abbey entrance and continue to the green footpath signs.
Turn right, marked 'Doorstep' walk. Keep the ruins to the right and
climb over a stile to cross the fast-running stream and past a small
waterfall. Follow the path over some stepping stones. Then walk with
the lake on the left and follow the winding path back to the car park.

An access path is marked on the information board. This seems to
run from the entry gate, past the ruins, and into the grassy land beyond.
In wet weather the ground could be soft.

Facilities
Free parking 0600-1830. WC+disabled when the Abbey (English
Heritage) is open.

Getting there

From Junction 4 take the A18, Doncaster and Doncaster Racecourse direction. Follow signs to the racecourse and turn left into Gate 8 from Leger Way. Continue to the car park at the end of the lane.

Return to M18 Junction 4

Turn right from Gate 8 and take the A18, Thorpe road at the next three roundabouts. At the fourth roundabout, take exit 3, A630 Scunthorpe. Continue to return to the M18.

The walk

Sandall Beat Wood is much bigger than it seems, with dozens of criss-crossing paths inviting walkers to explore the woods.

Follow the main track from the car park, and turn left for the visitor centre and facilities. There's a sturdy play area for kids here, with lots to climb and slide on.

The wood continues beyond the playground, either over a footbridge or by heading away from the visitor centre on one of the many paths.

Facilities

Free car park. WC. Access paths. Children's play area.

Waterside DN8 4JQ

Getting there
From Junction 6 turn into Waterside Road (a No Through Road);
northbound exit 1, southbound exit 4. Bear left to park in the John Bull
Inn car park, or in one of the roadside parking bays.

Return to M18 Junction 6
Leave the village along Waterside Road and rejoin the motorway at the
roundabout.

The walk
Walk past the front of the pub and continue along the short lane. At the
last house take a track to the right of a post and then turn right at a stile
and footpath sign. Walk with the water to your right along a pleasant,
grassy track, crossing a couple more stiles. (All of the stiles have
spaces for dogs to get
round or under.)

At the end of the
watery ditch, walk up the
bank on the right and
turn right on a raised path
along the side of a large
flood plain. Stay on this
path until the end of the
village and a five-bar gate.
Go over the stile and turn
right onto a track and back
to The John Bull.

Thomas Crapper was
born in Waterside, and
adverts for his early water
closet designs adorn the walls of the
pub.

Facilities
At The John Bull Inn (01405 814677)
pub food is served 1200-1400, Tues-
Sun. Well-behaved dogs welcome in
the bar. Campervan access.

M20

From London to Folkestone, via Ashford

Junction

2	Trosley Country Park
4	Manor Park Country Park
7	Thurnham
9	King's Wood

Trosley Country Park DA13 0SG

Getting there
From Junction 2 follow signs to the A227, Meopham and Wrotham.
Turn right off the A227 signed Trosley Country Park. Turn right,
Waterlow Road, signed Trosley Park and Tea Rooms. After about 60m,
turn right into the park entrance.

Return to M20 Junction 2
Turn left out of the park, then left again at Waterlow Road. Turn left,
A227, and return to the M20.

The walk
Trosley Park was formerly part of the Trosley Towers Estate, and is 160
acres of woodland and chalk downland. Look out for rare plants and
animals here, such as the musk orchid and the chalkhill blue butterfly.

Three walks of varying lengths and terrain are marked with
colour-coded posts. The red walk is flat, and takes around 60 minutes.
The blue walk is hilly and steep in places. The yellow walk offers easy
access.

Facilities
P&D car parks. WC+disabled. Refreshments, maps and information
board. Dog warden on duty. Campervan access.

Getting there

From Junction 4 follow signs to West Malling, Rochester. At a
roundabout take exit 1, A228
Tonbridge. At the traffic lights
turn right, A20, signed West
Malling. At a roundabout turn
left, West Malling. Go through
the town centre; the signed
entrance to Manor Park is on
the left.

Return to M20 Junction 4

Turn right from the park and
through West Malling town
centre. At the roundabout take
exit 2, A20 Maidstone. At the
traffic lights turn left, A228 Rochester road. Turn left, A228, and join the
M20 at the next roundabout.

The walk

There's one marked footpath through copses of trees, wide grassy
areas, and a lake in this spacious aristo-park, once part of an 18th
century estate created by Thomas Douce.

Look out for the rare breed
cattle that graze here, and, as
this is a nature conservation site,
you may also get to see some
less familiar birds and plants.

Facilities

P&D car park closes at dusk.
WC+disabled. Small café.
Children's play area. Map and
information board. Campervan
access. Shops for picnic
supplies in West Malling.

Thurnham ME14 3LD

Getting there

From Junction 7 follow signs to Maidstone. At a roundabout take exit 1, Bearsted, and exit 1 at the next roundabout. Turn left, Hockers Lane, and enter Detling. At a Post Office turn right – Thurnham. At Thurnham, park at The Black Horse Inn, non-patrons with permission from reception.

Return to M20 Junction 7

Turn left out of the car park and drive to Detling. At the centre of the village turn left into The Street. Drive over the motorway and turn right at a crossroads. Take exit 2 at following two roundabouts and rejoin the M20.

The walk

Turn left, Thurnham Lane, and walk uphill. Turn left at a stile on the left, White Horse Wood. Take a diagonal route downhill to cross a stile, and turn right to a wooden kissing gate on the right. Turn left down the hill and cross over a lane (Pilgrims' Way) into the field ahead; a pole marks the spot. Follow the path diagonally to the left to a church. Walk through the churchyard and turn left at the lane and back to The Black Horse.

Facilities

The 18th century Black Horse Inn (01622 737185) is open from 1200. Well-behaved dogs on leads welcome at bookable 'dog' table. Campervan access.

Getting there

From Junction 9 follow the A251, Faversham. Keep straight at the next four roundabouts on the A251, and turn left at the traffic lights signed A251, Faversham. Continue for 3.5 miles, then take a sharp right turn into the King's Wood car park.

Return to M20 Junction 9

Turn left towards Ashford A251. After 3.5 miles, turn right at the traffic lights signed M20, Ashford. Take exit 2 at the next three roundabouts, and exit 3 at the next roundabout and return to the M20.

The walk

Footpaths are clearly marked throughout the 1500 acres of King's Wood, with a choice of routes of between one and five miles.

For the 3 mile 'Beech Walk,' take the signed path to the left of the picnic area to follow the meandering paths through the ancient forest, and enjoy the leafy views across the valleys.

This was once a royal hunting forest, and herds of deer still remain. You are more likely to see sculptures than deer, though, as this is the main site of the Stour Valley Arts Project.

Facilities

Free parking. Information board with routes. Campervan access.

London Orbital

Junction	
3	Farningham Woods Nature Reserve
6	Marden Park
8	Banstead Heath
9	Ashtead Common
10	Ockham Common
13	Runnymede Pleasure Grounds
18	Chorleywood Common
20	Grand Union Canal
23	South Mimms Services
24	Trent Park
28	Weald Country Park
29	Thorndon Country Park
31	Belhus Woods Country Park

Getting there

From Junction 3 take the A20, West Kingsdown. Continue on this road at the next roundabout. At the next roundabout take the A225, Dartford. Drive under the motorway and turn left on Calfstock Lane (single track). The car park is at the end of the lane.

Return to M25 Junction 3

Return along Calfstock Lane and turn right, A225. At two successive roundabouts take exit 3, A20 Swanley, and rejoin the M25.

The walk

This is a gentle woodland walk in a nature reserve that is a haven of meditative calm.

An easy-to-follow, 1.6-mile circular walk is marked, and the paths are clear and well maintained. On entering the wood there's virtually no sign of human existence. Lovely.

Facilities

Free parking at woods. Campervan access. In Farningham village, The Lion Hotel (01322 860621; DA4 0DP) is a country pub serving food 1200-2130. Dogs welcome in large garden, water bowls provided.

Marden Park

Getting there
From Junction 6 take the A22, East Grinstead. At a roundabout take exit 1, Oxted, Westerham A25. Take the first left, Tandridge Hill Lane. Continue as the lane becomes single track. At a T-junction, turn left and there's a small, off-road parking area immediately to the right.

Return to M25 Junction 6
Return down Tandridge Hill Lane. Turn right at the T-junction, A25. Take exit 3, London, at the roundabout, and continue to the M25.

The walk
The North Downs Way runs through Marden Wood but, for a shorter stroll, take any path from the parking area leading downhill through the woods to a lush, grassy meadow.

The paths here are easy to follow, and the birdsong and wildlife rustlings in this unspoiled wood are a delight.

Marden Park was once owned by the orchestral conductor Sir Adrian Boult, and is now maintained by the Woodland Trust.

Facilities
None at Marden Park.

Getting there
From Junction 8 take the A217, London, Sutton. Continue on the A217 over a roundabout and turn left, signed Mogador, Stubbs Lane. Continue through a crossroads, signed Mogador and Banstead Heath. Bear right and park in the rear car park at The Sportsman.

Return to M25 Junction 8
Reverse the route to the A217 and turn left. Proceed to a roundabout, approximately 0.5 miles, to U-turn and return to the motorway from the A217.

The walk
There are waymarked paths across the Heath, and the area is popular with riders and walkers alike.

Banstead Heath is part of the extensive Banstead Downs, and forms part of the green 'lung' around London. There is

a mixture of open heath and woodland, and generally flat walking. There is so much space that the Heath is a delight to ramble around.

Facilities
The Sportsman (01737 246655) is a gastro-pub serving meals and snacks. Dogs on leads welcome inside and out. Campervan access. Several petrol stations on both sides of the A217.

Ashtead Common KT22 0DP

Getting there
From Junction 9 take the A243, London. Pass the Leatherhead Golf Club and park at The Star on the left.

Return to M25 Junction 9
Turn right onto the A243 and return to the M25.

The walk
Ashtead Common is an enormous 500 acres, and will easily satisfy the most energetic of walkers.

Cross the A243 at the refuge. Bear right and turn left at a Public Right of Way sign to Ashtead Common. A circular route through the woodland is marked on an information board at the entrance. The footpaths begin through brushwood entries and lead through glades of old oaks and abundant greenery.

Facilities
At The Star (01372 842416) meals and snacks are served from 1200. Free Wi-Fi, children's activities. Dogs allowed in the bar and beer garden. Campervan access.

Getting there

From Junction 10 take the A3, Guildford, Portsmouth. Get into the left-hand lane, and turn left immediately after a pedestrian bridge, signed Ockham Common. Enter the car park on the left.

Return to M25 Junction 10

Return to the A3, turning left onto the dual carriageway. Proceed until the first slip road exit and make a U-turn at the roundabout to return to the A3 (London) and M25.

The walk

Ockham Common is a site of special scientific interest, as well as a popular destination for families and dog walkers. Forest maps and walking routes are available at the refreshment kiosk in the car park.

Dog walkers will appreciate the Link Path from the car park to Boldermere Lake, crossing the road to walk over meadows to the water. Fishing is forbidden at the lake, so water-loving dogs can splash without restraint.

Facilities

Free parking to 1800. WC+disabled. Refreshment kiosk. Maps. Campervan access.

walking THE DOG

Runnymede Pleasure GroundsTW20 0AE

Getting there
From Junction 13 take the A30, Egham. Stay in the left lane (A30) and loop under the motorway. At the next roundabout take exit 3, A308 Windsor. Turn right, signed Pleasure Grounds, to enter the car park.

Return to M25 Junction 13
Turn left out of the car park. At the roundabout take first exit signed M25 to return to the motorway.

The walk
This is a large, bucolic city green with much to offer. On a warm summer's day expect to see families enjoying picnics underneath gazebos and tents. Children are well catered for with a brightly-painted, old-fashioned merry-go-round and bouncy castle.

From the car park, head towards the river to join the Thames Path national trail. This is part of a trail that runs alongside the Thames from its source to the sea.

Facilities
P&D parking. WC+disabled. Café. Children's playground. River boat trips. Campervan access.

Getting there
Leave the M25 at Junction 18 and take the A404, signed Chorleywood and Amersham. Shortly after the signed turning to a cemetery on the right, turn left into the unsigned car park.

Return to M25 Junction 18
Leave the car park and turn right. Continue to rejoin the M25.

The walk
There's excellent walking on this ancient common, with plenty of space for the travel-weary dog to spread his paws and fly into the bracken.

Follow the path from the car park and wander at will in the grassy spaces and woodland on the clear paths.

Now part of the Chilterns Area of Outstanding Beauty, the Common was mentioned in the Domesday Book.

Facilities
Free car park, with height restrictions. At the nearby Rose & Crown Inn (01923 283841) lunch is served from 1200. Well-behaved dogs welcome in the bar and beer garden.

Grand Union Canal WD4 8RE

Getting there
From Junction 20 take the A41, London NW and Watford. At the traffic lights turn left, signed Abbots Langley. The Waterside is on the left, just after a canal bridge.

Return to M25 Junction 20
Turn left from The Waterside car park. Turn right at the traffic lights, signed A41 Hemel Hempstead, and follow this road to return to the M25.

The walk
Turn left from the car park to cross the canal bridge, and access the towing path down the steep paths on each side of the bridge.

Turn left at a yellow footpath arrow to walk in the direction of Birmingham. This is the Grand Union Canal Walk. Pass a winding hole, where the sight of a narrowboat turning round can entertain, and continue as the path becomes more and more rural. Turn around at your halfway point to return to The Waterside.

Facilities
The Waterside (01923 262307) has an Italian menu, and food is served from 1200. Children's play area. Dogs welcome in the large garden, and outdoor covered area. Campervan access.

Getting there
Follow signs to South Mimms Services and park by the Day's Inn Motel.

Return to M25 Junction 23
Follow signs to the M25.

The walk
A path between the motel and services building leads to the Wash Lane Common nature reserve. Turn left and walk to a metal gate, and enter a field at a Public Bridleway sign. Turn right, with the hedge on your right, and walk around two sides of the field. Ignore a right turn and continue on the footpath. Climb a stile ahead and walk through the next field. Turn around here for a 30 minute walk.

Facilities
Welcome Break motorway facilities. Waitrose, Burger King, Coffee Primo, Eat-In, KFC. Children's play area. Campervan access.

Trent Park EN4 0PS

Getting there

From Junction 24 take the A111, Cockfosters and continue past West Lodge Hotel. After the tourist sign for 'Trent Country Park (300 yards),' look for the entrance on the left, just after a bend, through an imposing but unmarked gateway.

Return to M25 Junction 24

Turn right from the park entrance to the A111 and return to the M25 as signed.

The walk

This is an orderly and well-tended country park, with hard surface paths creating accessibility routes and clean, all-weather walking. The London Loop starts by the car park, and the route is shown on an informative notice board.

There is plenty of space to go off-path and enjoy the shade of the ancient spreading trees in this generously-sized estate.

Facilities

Free parking 0830 to dusk. WC+disabled. Visitor centre. Café with outdoor seating. Picnic tables. Water garden and children's activities. Campervan access.

Getting there

From Junction 28 take the A1023, Brentwood. Turn left almost immediately, signed South Weald. In the village of South Weald bear left, Weald Road; the entrance to the car park is signed to the right.

Return to M25 Junction 28

Turn left out of the car park onto Weald Road. Bear right in South Weald. At the A1023 turn right. The M25 intersection is directly ahead.

The walk

With nearly 500 acres of parkland, including lakes and avenues of mature trees, Weald Park is an attractive place to ramble.

There are no formal walking trails, just a huge amount of green space. Wildlife flourishes in these undisturbed surroundings, and deer can often be spotted at dusk.

Facilities

P&D car park. WC+disabled. Refreshments. Visitor centre – hours vary. All-Terrain Tramper Scooter hire from visitor centre (01277 261343). Campervan access.

Thorndon Country Park CM13 3RZ

Getting there
From Junction 29 take the A127, Basildon, Southend. Turn left for the A128, Brentwood road. Pass through Herongate and Ingrave, and turn left at the tourist signpost to Thorndon Country Park North, The Avenue.

Return to M25 Junction 29
Return to the A128, turning right from The Avenue. At the roundabout, take the A127 Romford to rejoin the M25 at the next roundabout.

The walk
There are two signed routes. The Wildside Walk (yellow signs) is a 5-mile route around the park. To reach the start point, follow the bridleway from the car park and turn left at the lake. At the Wildside Walk marker bear left to follow the signs. On the return leg, remember to turn left on the Bridleway to get back to the car park.

A shorter option is to take the bridleway from the car park, through the Octagon Plantation, and then turn right on the public footpath (red markers). Carry on to the boundary of the wood, and turn left. Pass through woodland, continuing straight at the crossroads of paths, to the Old Park. Then turn left onto a path shared with the Wildside Walk, until returning to the Bridleway. Pass the lake to the left on the return to the car park.

Facilities
P&D car park. WC+disabled. Visitor centre. Picnic tables. Refreshments. Shop, map and information board. Campervan access.

Getting there

From Junction 31, and at the roundabout, take the Aveley exit, Ship Lane. In Aveley turn left at a mini roundabout (High Street). At the next mini roundabout turn right, Mill Road. At next roundabout take exit 2, Upminster. After a mile turn right into Belhus Woods Country Park.

Return to M25 Junction 31

Turn left from the car park and take exit 2 at the roundabout to return to Aveley. Turn left at the first mini roundabout to the High Street, and right at the next mini roundabout onto Ship Lane. Continue to Junction 31. Follow signs to the M25 Gatwick (southbound) or Dartford Crossing A282 (northbound).

The walk

Formerly a country estate, the woodland is restful and tranquil.

Three walk routes are signed around the park. The Blue route is 2km, the Brown route 2.5km and the Red route 3km. All routes begin through the gates near the visitor centre.

An information board gives a huge amount of detail about each track, including its steepness. The Blue route is flat, with a wide accessible track.

Facilities

P&D car park, tax exempt vehicles free, open 0800-dusk. WC. Visitor centre. Light refreshments. Campervan access.

From New Forest to Portsmouth

Junction

Getting there
From Junction 2 take the A36, Salisbury. At the next roundabout
continue on the A36 (there are services on this roundabout). Enter
Wellow. Turn left, signed Bramshaw, Black Hill Road. Cross a cattle grid
and the car park is on the left.

Return to M27 Junction 2
Turn right out of the car park. At the T-junction turn right –
Southampton A36. At the roundabout take exit 3, signed Southampton,
M27, to rejoin the motorway.

The walk
Walk onto the Common from the car park to a wide swathe of grass
between the trees and bracken. There are no marked paths, and no
navigational difficulties in heading away from the road into the lush
woodland. As a general indication, bear right rather than left to stay
clear of the nearby golf and cricket areas.

There's scope here for a long walk if time and weather permit.

Facilities
Free parking. Campervan access. Services on the A36 roundabout, with
WC, café, petrol.

walking THE DOG

Itchen Valley Country Park SO30 3HQ

Getting there

From Junction 5 take the A335, Southampton; then turn left at the traffic lights. At a roundabout take exit 2, Mansbridge Road. At the next roundabout take exit 1, Allington Lane. Continue to Itchen Valley Country Park, which is on the left.

Return to M27 Junction 5

Turn right out of the park. At the mini roundabout go straight on. At the next roundabout take exit 3, A27 Eastleigh direction. Enter Southampton and at the next roundabout take exit 2, Eastleigh. Turn right at the traffic lights, signed London A335 and return to the M27.

The walk

There are five marked trails in the park to satisfy the needs of walkers, all starting from the visitor centre.

The 30 minute Paw Trail is designed for dogs. It's a leafy, well-maintained path that includes a large open area for ball games. The Forest Trail is an easy access path. Other trails of varying lengths meander through the 400 acres of parkland.

Facilities

P&D car park 0830 to dusk. WC+disabled. Café. Visitor centre. Children's play area. Electric scooter hire from visitor centre. Dog poo bags (10p) from visitor centre. Campervan access.

motorway walks for drivers and dogs

Manor Farm Country Park SO31 1BH

Getting there
From Junction 8 follow signs to Manor Farm Country Park. Take the second right turn, Rylands Lane, to enter the park.

Return to M27 Junction 8
Leave the grounds of the park and turn left, signed M27, and return to the motorway.

The walk
With four car parks and many walk routes, Manor Farm is worth several visits.

From the farm and visitor centre car park, walk to a footpath sign by the entrance. Two paths start from this point: one is the Barnsfield path, which leads to refreshments and a river; the other path, marked with a red arrow, is a rural route running between fields, and it's up to you to decide how far you want to go and then turn around.

Dog walkers not visiting the farm are encouraged to use one of the earlier car parks.

Facilities
Parking charge on entry. Working farm admission separate. WC+disabled. Café. Visitor centre. Picnic area. Working farm museum. Children's activities. Dog water. Accessible trails. Maps available from entry point and visitor centre. Campervan access.

Botley Wood PO15 7LJ

Getting there
From Junction 9 follow signs to Whiteley, Outlet Shopping. At a roundabout take exit 2, signed Outlet Shopping, Whiteley Way. Enter the Shopping Village and park near the entrance.

Return to M27 Junction 9
Leave the shopping village and take exit 2 at the roundabout, signed M27, and rejoin the motorway at the next roundabout.

The walk
Leave the shopping village and cross to the other side of the roundabout to a blue pedestrian sign. Turn right on a tarmac path across a small bridge, then left onto a gravel track.

Turn right at a waymark post, covered in yellow arrows and mostly hidden behind a hawthorn bush. Follow this wide track to enter Whiteley Pastures. Once here, it is as if the outlet village never existed.

This woodland is home to Hampshire's largest nightingale population, so keep your ears open for its distinctive song. Follow the track for half your walk time, and return the same way.

Facilities
Free parking. Shopping facilities, including picnic supplies and ATMs. Guide Dogs only in the shopping areas. Pet dogs are welcome on the terrace of Frankie and Benny, close to the entrance. Campervan access.

M40

From London to Birmingham, via Oxford

Junction

2	Burnham Beeches
4	Spade Oak Nature Reserve
5	Cowleaze Woods
6	Cuxham
7	Great Haseley (northbound)
9	Weston on the Green
11	Middleton Cheney
15	Hatton Locks
16	Henley-in-Arden (southbound)

Burnham Beeches

Getting there
From Junction 2 take the A355, Slough. Enter Farnham Common and take the 3rd right turn after an infant school – Beeches Road. Go straight at a crossroads to enter Burnham Beeches car park.

Return to M40 Junction 2
Return to the A355 and then turn left to rejoin the motorway.

The walk
Burnham Beeches gives West Londoners a recreation space in 540 acres of ancient woodland.

One short route is to go straight through the trees from the car park as far as the Withy Spring, following a clear path to cross the stream. At an intersection of paths turn right. Cross Sir Henry Peter's Drive and continue in the same direction to cross 'The Heath.' This path leads down to the Upper Pond. Bear right on one of the many paths to return to the car park.

The wheelchair-accessible path begins at the information point, where full route details are available.

Facilities
Free parking. WC+disabled. Café, and ice cream van in summer. Information centre with maps and walk routes. Campervan access.

Getting there

From Junction 4 take the A404, Marlow. Bear left, A4155, signed
Marlow, Bourne End and continue to Little Marlow. Enter Bourne End
and turn right, Coldmoorholme Lane, to reach The Spade Oak car park.

Return to M40 Junction 4

Turn right from the car park. At the T-junction, turn left. Take exit 1 at
the mini roundabout. Continue to a roundabout and take exit 3, A4010
Aylesbury, to return to the M40.

The walk

This is a 45 minute circular walk without stiles.

From the car park turn right and then left at a public footpath sign.
Follow the footpath arrow to the right before a metal kissing gate. Walk
parallel to the lane for a short distance.

Cross a wooden footbridge and turn left at the next footpath sign.
Walk through one field with the hedge on your left and into the next
field. Follow the path into woodland on the left. Cross a metal footbridge
and take the yellow permissive path to the left. At the lake turn left.

Shortly after a picnic table and lifebuoy follow a yellow marker over
a footbridge to the left. Cross a field, and go through the kissing gate to
return to The Spade Oak.

Facilities

At The Spade Oak (01628 520090) food is served from 1200. Well-
behaved dogs on leads are welcome in the unpaved garden area.

walking THE DOG

Cowleaze Woods

Getting there
From Junction
5 take the A40,
Stokenchurch.
Immediately
turn left, signed
A40 Lewknor,
Oxford. Turn left,
signed Christmas
Common. Turn left
into the Cowleaze
Woods Forestry
Commission car
park.

**Return to M40
Junction 5**
Turn right from
the car park. At the junction turn right – A40 – and
continue to return to the M40.

The walk
Walk away from the road on one of the many paths to
a broad grassy stretch, which seems to be the playground of choice for
many local dogs.
    Within the wood there are many paths to choose from to enjoy a
very satisfying, 30-40 minute ramble. In spring, Cowleaze Woods is
awash with bluebells.

Facilities
Free parking; 6ft 6 height restriction. At The Leathern Bottle (01844
351482; OX49 5TW) in nearby Lewknor. food is served 1200-1400,
reservations recommended at weekends. Children's play area, beer
garden. Dogs are welcome in the pub; dog water provided.

Getting there

From Junction 6 take the B4009, signed Watlington. Pass through
Shipburn and enter Watlington. At a T-junction turn right, B480
Cuxham. At a roundabout take exit 2, unsigned. Enter Cuxham and park
at The Half Moon on the right. The car park is gated.

Return to M40 Junction 6

Turn left from the car park and enter Watlington. Take exit 2 at the
roundabout. At a Give Way sign turn left, signed High Wycombe. Turn
left, B4009 signed Chinnor and M40, to rejoin the motorway.

The walk

Turn right out of the car park and turn left at a green footpath sign to
Manor Farm. Continue up the hill on this farm track, which gets steeper
as you go.

This is a one-track walk, so
continue with the hedge on the right
and fields on each side for half your
walk time, then return the same way.

Facilities

At The Half Moon
(01491 614151),
a 17th century
traditional
thatched inn,
well-behaved
dogs are
welcome inside
and in the
garden. Disabled
access buzzer.
Campervan
access.

Great Haseley OX44 7JQ   Northbound only

Getting there
From Junction 7 take the A329, Wallingford. Turn left, signed Great Haseley. In Great Haseley turn right, signed Great Milton, Rectory Road. Park at The Plough Inn on the left.

Return to M40 northbound
Turn right from the car park and left at the T-junction signed Thame. At the next T-junction – unsigned – turn right. Turn left, signed Birmingham M40, Oxford A40. At a roundabout take exit 2 and continue to rejoin the M40.

The walk
Turn left out of the car park and walk to a green footpath arrow sign by Horseclose Cottages. Follow this arrow, cross an access road and continue into a field onto a well-trodden path. Continue through a gate and across a road towards a church. Proceed through the churchyard and turn left at the arrow.

At a recreation ground carry straight on and continue into the next field for an entirely rural romp in the Chilterns. Continue to follow the arrows for as long as you wish, then turn around to retrace the route. Great Haseley has featured more than once in the *Midsomer Murders* TV series.

Facilities
At The Plough (01844 279283) food is served from 1200. Dogs welcome in the bar. Campervan access. Oxford motorway services are on the return route.

Getting there

From Junction 9 take the A34, Oxford, then turn left, signed Middleton Stoney B430. Drive over the dual carriageway, and at a mini roundabout turn left, signed motorway. Park at The Chequers Country Inn on the right.

Return to M40 Junction 9

Turn right out of the car park, and then left onto the dual carriageway, signed A34, M40, to return to the motorway.

The walk

Climb a stile to the rear of the bar entrance to enter a field. Walk with the car park fence on your left, and when this runs out turn right. Continue to a gate with a yellow waymarker and through a copse in a half left direction to a kissing gate. Bear slightly left across a field to a metal gate in the far corner. Cross a wooden footbridge and then follow the arrow half right into a field. Head for the wooden gate ahead, where a further arrow points into woodland to the left. Turning around at a wooden footbridge gives a 30 minute walk.

Facilities

At The Chequers (01869 351743) food is served from 1200. Well-behaved dogs on leads are welcome in the bar and garden. Campervan access.

Middleton Cheney OX17 2ND

Getting there
From Junction 11 take the A422, Brackley. At the roundabout take
exit 3, A422 Buckingham, Milton Keynes. Turn left, signed Middleton
Cheney. Park at The New Inn on the left.

Return to M40 Junction 11
Return to the A422 and turn right, signed Banbury. Continue on the
A422 to return to the M40.

The walk
Turn right from the car park to a footpath sign to Thenford, and walk
down a paved driveway. Climb a stile at the footpath sign on the left and
proceed with Middleton Farm on your right. Cross the next stile and
head towards the trees.

Climb another stile and follow the arrow slightly to the right across
two fields. Go through a gate and stile to follow the arrow pointing to
the right. Turn left at the corner of the field and go through a metal gate.
Turn left and immediately left again through a gate into a copse with a
pool. Turn around here for a 35 minute walk.

Facilities
At The New Inn (01295 710399) meals and snacks are served
1200-1430. Well-behaved dogs welcome in the bar. Campervan access.

Getting there

From Junction 15 take the A46, Coventry. Turn left, Solihull A4177, and continue to Hatton. Turn left on a hill, signed Hatton Locks and car park.

Return to M40 Junction 15

From the car park turn right. At the roundabout take exit 2, A4177 Warwick. At the next roundabout, take exit 3 A46, signed M40, Birmingham, and rejoin the M40 at the Longbridge roundabout.

The walk

Cross the canal bridge and turn right onto the Grand Union canal for a glorious walk along the towpath, and the chance to watch narrowboats climbing the 21, closely-placed locks of the 'Stairway to Heaven,' or Hatton Flight.

Pass the café and shop on the left and walk past two winding holes as far as Bridge No 55, which is a good turning point for a 30 minute walk.

Facilities

P&D car park open 0900-1700. WC. Café with outdoor seating, shop. Campervan access. The Waterman (01926 492427) offers an all-day menu from 1200. Dogs welcome in the bar and large garden.

Henley in Arden B95 5GD   Southbound only

Getting there
Exit at Junction 16 and turn right. Continue to Henley in Arden, A3400. At the end of the town turn left, Warwick Road, and turn left after a petrol station, Prince Harry Drive, to a car park.

Return to M40 Junction 16 southbound
Turn left at the end of Prince Harry Drive, Warwick Road. Continue through Claverdon village, and turn right where signed to the M40 at the Longbridge roundabout.

The walk
Pass a children's play area and cross a metal footbridge. Turn left towards a church, and then right through a kissing gate. Walk uphill and bear left to walk parallel to the churchyard, through a copse of trees and downhill to join a path at the

bottom of the slope. Turn right and circle around the foot of The Mount, a motte and bailey site, for a 30 minute walk.

Facilities
There are many 16th century hostelries and cafes on Henley High Street, most with outdoor seating in summer. Also a supermarket and delis for picnic fare.

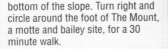

The Blue Bell (01564 793049; B95 5QP) is a gastro-pub that serves meals and bar snacks from midday, Tues-Sun. Dogs welcome in the bar and at outside tables.

M42

Birmingham semi-orbital

Junction

Lickey Hills B45 8ER   Westbound only

Getting there
From Junction 1 take the B4096, Rednal and Lickey, exit 4. Continue for just over a mile, pass a Texaco garage, and turn right at the Lickey Hills sign, Warren Lane.

Return to M5 Junction 4
From Warren Lane turn left on the B4096. Drive back to the M42 roundabout and take the 4th exit – Birmingham A46, M5. Continue on the A46 to join the M5 at Junction 4.

The walk
There are three trails at the Lickey Hills. The Squirrel Trail is the shortest at just under a mile, the Bluebell Trail is 1.5 miles, and the Woodpecker Trail an enthusiastic 7 miles. All the trails are clearly marked and very easy to follow.

The Lickeys were J R R Tolkien's inspiration for Middle Earth in *The Lord of the Rings,* and he is said to have known every inch of the landscape, trees and plants here.

Facilities
Free car park, closes at dusk. WC. Visitor centre. Shop. Café with outdoor seating, large children's play area and child-friendly displays about the park. Campervan access.

Getting there

From Junction 4 take the A3400, Henley-in-Arden road. Turn right at a roundabout, signed Illshaw Heath, Kineton Lane. At a T-junction turn right, signed Earlswood, Cut-Throat Lane. Turn right, signed Earlswood. At a crossroads, turn left and immediately right to park at The Reservoir Hotel.

Return to M42 Junction 4

Turn left from the car park, and immediately right. Bear left into Cut-Throat Lane. Take the third left turn, and continue to Kineton Lane. At the roundabout, take exit 1 A3400, Solihull, and return to the M42.

The walk

This walk takes you around the perimeter of the Windmill Pool, and is flat, easy walking.

Leave the car park and turn left into Valley Road. Turn left at a wooden kissing gate. Follow the path around the lake and turn around after 15-20 minutes for a 30 to 40 minute walk. Note that the lake is not safe for dog swimming.

Facilities

At The Reservoir (01564 702220) food is served from midday (a budget menu with the focus on families). Children's play area and Wacky Warehouse (entry charge). Dogs allowed at just one tiny patio table overlooking the car park. Campervan access.

walking THE DOG

Kingsbury Water Park B76 0DY

Getting there

From Junction 9 take the A4097, signed Kingsbury Water Park. At the roundabout, take exit 1 (Coton Road). Continue ahead, and the entrance to Kingsbury Water Park is signed on the right.

Return to M42 Junction 9

Turn left out of the car park, and at the roundabout take exit 3. Continue ahead to return to the motorway.

The walk

This park is a planning miracle, created out of spent gravel pits. There are fifteen lakes in 620 acres of leisure space, and many of the paths are surfaced, so it's fine, all-weather and accessible walking.

Maps and info available from the visitor centre, but essentially this is somewhere where it is very comfortable to amble around the lakes and woodland without a fixed plan or route.

Facilities

P&D car park open 0830 to dusk. WC+disabled. Visitor centre. Café. Shop. Adventure playground. Picnic site. Miniature railway. Access paths. Mobility scooter hire (01827 872660). Campervan access.

Getting there
From Junction 11 take the Measham exit. Turn right, signed Appleby Magna, Rectory Lane. At a T-junction with Measham Road, turn right into Church Street. Pass a church, and park at The Black Horse on the right.

Return to M42 Junction 11
Pass the church and turn left into Rectory Lane. At the T-junction turn left, and rejoin the motorway at the next roundabout.

The walk
Turn onto Black Horse Hill and turn right at a footpath sign to the left of 'Apple Tree House.' Keep a hedge on your right and continue to the corner of the field,

passing a couple of yellow footpath arrows.

Follow a blue arrow to the left, through a gate, and then half left through the centre of the crops in the field ahead. Follow a yellow arrow through a gap in the hedgerow, and then turn left into the next field, heading toward a yellow marker ahead. Cross a small footbridge to enter the next field, and follow the path through the crop.

At the end of the field aim for a yellow-topped post and turn left on Black Horse Hill to return to the pub.

Facilities
At the 16th century Black Horse (01530 270588) lunch is served from midday, except Mondays. Dogs welcome in the bar, and at the outdoor tables. Campervan access.

Welsh Borders and the Severn Estuary

M48
Junction

1	Severn View Services
2	Tintern Abbey

M50
Junction

1	Twyning
2	Dymock
3	Dymock Forest
4	Wilton

Getting there
Access Severn View Services as signed from the motorway.

Return to M48 Junction 1
Return to the motorway as signed.

The walk
Severn View services sit right on the long distance Severn Way path, so this walk couldn't be easier to fit into your journey.

Walk past the Travelodge to skirt the base of a grassy knoll, towards an office building and a waymark post. Turn right into woodland. Follow the path downward and round to the right.

At a wooden kissing gate go straight, into a field, with the River Severn on your left, to the next kissing gate. There's a good view of the estuary and Severn Bridge from here.

Walk through the next field, with a small tower to the right. From here the line of the path is clear to see as it drops down a small but steep hill to the next gate. Continue on this path, always with the river to the left, until your halfway point, then turn around to return.

Facilities
Moto motorway services. Dogs allowed at outside tables. Campervan access.

walking THE DOG

Tintern Abbey NP16 6TE

Getting there
From Junction 2 take the A466, Chepstow, and continue on this route to Tintern Abbey and car park.

Return to M48 Junction 2
Turn left from the car park and continue on the A466 to return to the motorway.

The walk
Walk towards the river and turn left, with the river to your right. Follow the signed Tintern Trail footpath to cross a footbridge over the river and turn right. The path from here is a broad swathe of green meadowland. Reverse the route to return to Tintern Abbey.

Facilities
At Tintern Abbey, free car park for pub and tearoom customers. Public WC+disabled. The Anchor (01291 689207) serves food and snacks all day. Small general stores in tearooms. Well-behaved dogs on leads welcome in the large garden areas.

The Abbey is open 0930-1730. Entry charge. Only assistance dogs are permitted inside the ruins. Campervan access.

Getting there
From Junction 1 follow signs to Twyning. Enter Twyning and park in The Fleet Inn car park.

Return to M50 Junction 1
Turn right from the car park and rejoin the M50 as signed.

The walk
Turn left from the car park and walk down to the River Avon. Turn right at the river onto the marked river path, climbing over one stile at the beginning. Walk along the wide, grassy track with the river to the left to your halfway point, then turn around to return to the car park.

This is a perfect hot weather walk over cooling grass. Pleasure boats pass by from time to time, and the atmosphere is very relaxing.

Facilities
At the 15th century Fleet Inn (01684 274310) food is served from midday. Outside seating area overlooking the river. Children's playground. Well-behaved dogs on leads are welcome in the bar area. Campervan access.

Dymock GL18 2AG

Getting there

From Junction 2 take the A417, Ledbury. Turn left, signed Bromsberrow Heath, Beach Lane. Continue straight until a crossroads at Greenway, and turn left, B4216. Enter Dymock and park near The Beaumont Arms.

Return to M50 Junction 2

Turn left by the pub, signed Ledbury B4216. Turn right, signed Broome Green, Bromsberrow, and continue through these villages. At a T-junction turn right, signed M50, Gloucester A417, to return to the M50.

The walk

Join the waymarked Daffodil Way opposite the Beauchamp Arms. Walk through two wild flower meadows and over a small brook. Follow the path through a metal gate into a large farmed field. Turn left to walk around the field with the hedgerow to your left.

Continue on the broad track as far as the telephone wires and a clump of trees. For a 30-40 minute walk, turn around here. If time permits, there's an interesting display about the Dymock poets inside the church.

Facilities

The Beauchamp Arms (01531 890266) is a community-owned pub with bar food available 1200-1400, Tues-Sun. Dogs welcome in the back bar and at outside tables.

Getting there
From Junction 3 take the B4221, signed Newent, Gorsley. Turn left just after the Roadmaker Inn into Ivy House Lane. Take the second left turn, passing the 'The Larches.' At a T-junction turn left. The unsigned entrance to the Forestry Commission car park is on the right.

Return to M50 Junction 3
Turn left from the car park, and then turn right into Swagwater Lane. Turn right at a T-junction, and then right at the next T-junction by The Roadmaker Inn to return to the M50.

The walk
This is walking country at its best through Forestry Commission woodland. There are no signed trails, but the paths are clear and easy to follow.

The path from the right side of the car park gives a fine view over the valley and the wooded hills beyond. It's easy to lose all sense of time here, so if you have a schedule to keep to, set an alarm!

Facilities
Free car park in Dymock Forest. Campervan access. The Roadmaker Inn (01989 720352; HR9 7SW) in Gorsley is run by a team of Gurkhas, with Gurkha food a speciality. Open from midday. Dogs permitted at tables on the small outdoor patio.

walking THE DOG

Wilton HR9 6AQ

Getting there
Continue from the M50 on the
A40, Monmouth to the Wilton
roundabout. Turn left, signed B4260
Wilton. Take the first right, Wilton
Lane, before the bridge and park at
The White Lion.

Return to M50 Junction 4
To return to the M50, take exit 4,
A40, from the Wilton roundabout to
rejoin the motorway.

The walk
Walk along the lane for a short
distance, passing the Wilton Court
Hotel on the right, to a stile and
footpath sign on the left. Go over
the stile (with dog hole) and follow
the clear path along the river bank
over three fields. Then return the
same way.

Dog swimming is possible from
the rear garden of The White Lion,
where there is some protection from
the strong current of the River Wye.

Facilities
The White Lion (01989 562785) is
a popular, 17th century inn with a
good, Bistro-style menu. Well-
behaved dogs are welcome in the
bar and rear gardens. Campervan
access.

The northwest motorways

M56
From Manchester to Chester
Junction

2	Wythenshawe Park (southbound)
5	Styal Country Park
6	Lindow Common
7	Dunham Massey Hall
11	Walton Hall

M57
From the M62 to Liverpool North
Junction

1	Stadt Moers Country Park
4	Croxteth Hall & Country Park

M60
Manchester Orbital
Junction

6	Trafford Water Park
16	Clifton Country Park (southbound)
19	Heaton Park
20	Alkrington Woods (eastbound)
23	Daisy Nook Country Park
24	Reddish Vale Country Park
27	Woodbank Memorial Park (eastbound)

Wythenshawe Park M23 0BA   Southbound only

Getting there
From Junction 2 take exit 2, M6 Birmingham. At the next roundabout take exit 2, M6 Birmingham. At the next roundabout take exit 3, Wythenshawe Park and A5103. Merge and stay in the left-hand lane. At the traffic lights turn left, and then left at the sign for Wythenshawe Park. Drive through the grounds to reach the car park on the right.

Return to M56 southbound
Exit the park and turn right. Continue straight at the first and second traffic lights, signed M56 Chester, Warrington. Turn right onto the A5103, signed M56, Chester and follow the signs to return to the M56.

The walk
There are 250 acres of parkland here, so plenty of space for exercise in this island of calm amidst the transport network.

Cromwell's troops occupied this estate in the early 1600s, and there's now a statue of Cromwell near the hall. This marks the area where local dog owners seem to exercise their hounds.

Trails are not signed in the park, but helpful maps are available at the visitor centre.

Facilities
Free parking, WC+disabled. Café. Visitor centre, wardens on duty. Campervan access.

Getting there

Leave the M56 at Junction 5 following the motorway 'leg' and take exit 2 at the roundabout. At the next roundabout take exit 2, B5166 Cheadle, Styal Country Park. Then follow the brown tourist signs to Styal Country Park.

Return to M56 Junction 5

Exit the car park and turn right. Enter Wythenshawe, and turn left at the traffic lights, signed M56. At the roundabout take exit 1, signed M56/airport. At the next roundabout take exit 2 to return to the motorway.

The walk

A 19th century cotton mill is not the obvious place for a walk, but amongst the traces of industrial Manchester there are 380 acres of country park.

Leave the car park and go through a wooden kissing gate on the left; this is a waymarked footpath to Wilmslow. Follow the yellow arrows to cross the fields on a well-trodden path. Then reverse the route to return to the car park.

The National Trust exhibitions are worth a visit, but no dogs are permitted and there's restricted access for pushchairs.

Facilities

P&D car park, NT members free. WC. Restaurant. NT shop. Separate charges to visit the mill and exhibitions. Campervan access.

Lindow Common SK9 5LR

Getting there

From Junction 6 take the A538, Wilmslow. At the roundabout continue on this road. Pass The Boddington and Dragon and immediately turn right, then quickly left into the unsigned car park for Lindow Common.

Return to M56 Junction 6

Turn right from the car park and left at the T-junction, A538. At the roundabout take exit 1, M56, to return to the motorway.

The walk

There are well maintained paths leading into the heathland, and the most obvious path from the car park leads deliciously deeper into the heather.

This is an area to wander around at will, enjoying the feel of this timeless common land.

Lindow Moss, next to the Common, is famous for the Iron Age body preserved in its peat, but the marsh is not safe for walkers.

Facilities

Free parking. At the Boddington & Dragon Arms (01625 525849) food is served from midday. Children welcome until 2000. Dogs outside only. Wi-Fi access. Campervan access.

Getting there
From Junction 7 take the A56
Altrincham and Dunham Massey
road. At a roundabout take exit 3,
Dunham Massey. At the traffic lights
turn left, B5160, Charcoal Road.
Turn left as signed for Dunham
Massey Hall.

Return to M56
Exit Dunham Massey and turn
right. At the traffic lights turn right,
signed M56.

The walk
A National Trust property, Dunham
Massey Hall dominates its 250
acre park. Guided tours available,
exhibitions and Winter Garden.
Entry charges apply. Assistance
dogs are welcome in all parts of
the house and grounds.

A free walks leaflet is
provided, detailing the many trails
throughout the park grounds.

For dog walkers, the woods surrounding the picnic area have
been designated off-lead dog walking space. Dogs must be on a lead
elsewhere as deer roam throughout the park.

Facilities
P&D parking, NT members free, open 0900-1700. WC+disabled.
Restaurant. Kiosk. Picnic tables. NT shop. Wheelchair loan. Campervan
access.

walking THE DOG

Walton Hall WA4 6SN

Getting there
From Junction 11 take the A56
Warrington. Enter Walton. At the
traffic lights turn right, signed
Walton Hall and gardens. Turn
right at the Walton Arms and
continue to the car park.

Return to M56 Junction 11
Turn left at the Walton Arms.
At the traffic lights, turn left,
signed M56, Runcorn. At the
roundabout take exit 1, N. Wales
M56 and return to the motorway.

The walk
Walton Hall and gardens are
the main attraction for visitors,
and fully accessible paths and
facilities are found here. The
gardens are reached from the
left-hand side of the car park
entrance. Families flock here in
the school holidays to enjoy the
outdoor games, zoo and play
areas, or to ramble through the
extensive parkland.

The dog walk route lies outside the park, on the Bridgewater Canal
tow path adjoining the car park. Turn left to walk along the cool and
leafy path. This is considerably quieter than the hall, and an ideal stroll
for those seeking peace and quiet.

Facilities
P&D gated car park open 0800 to dusk. Visitor centre. WC+disabled.
Café. Gift shop. Children's activities. Campervan access.

Getting there
From Junction 1 turn to Whiston, eastbound exit 3, westbound exit 6.
At the traffic lights turn left, Huyton, and the unsigned entrance to Stadt
Moers Park is on the left before a bridge.

Return to M57 Junction 1
Turn right from the car park and turn right at the traffic lights, signed
Whiston Station. Continue to return to the motorway.

The walk
Stadt Moers Park has been regenerated from wasteland, and is now
a thriving natural environment with meadows, woodland and ponds,
criss-crossed by footpaths and spread over 220 acres. The paths are
clearly colour-coded and include circular routes suitable for buggies
and wheelchairs.
     To reach the main part of the park, go past the Environment Centre
and through a tunnel under the motorway to the starting point for all
the trails.

Facilities
Free parking. Visitor centre. WC+disabled (when visitor centre is open).
Campervan access.

walking THE DOG

Croxteth Hall and Country Park L12 0HB

Getting there
From Junction 4 take the A5207, St Helens. At traffic lights, turn left A580, Liverpool direction. At the next traffic lights turn left, West Derby, Stonebridge Lane. Continue through a housing development and turn right at the traffic lights. Turn left at a roundabout, and the gates to Croxteth Park are on the left.

Return to M57 Junction 4
Turn right from the park and then take exit 3 at the roundabout, Croxteth. At the traffic lights turn right A580, signed St Helens. Continue and follow M57 signs to return to the motorway.

The walk
Croxteth Hall sits in over 500 acres of parkland with miles of trails marked throughout the park.

The River Trail is a hard-surfaced, wheelchair- and buggy-friendly path that starts at the main Hall.

Facilities
Free parking. WC+disabled. Café. Children's play areas, Jungle Parc, adventure playground. Walled garden. Gift shop. Park opens 0700-2000 summer, 0700-1800 winter. Campervan access.

Getting there

From Junction 6 follow signs to Trafford Watersports. At a roundabout take exit 2, Trafford Water Park, and continue to the car park.

Return to M60 Junction 6

Leave the car park and return to the M60 as signed at the roundabouts.

The walk

There are three trails in Trafford Water Park, all well signed from the visitor centre. The first – Chorlton Water Park Trail – can be joined by walking down to the River Mersey and then turning right to follow the marked path (2 miles approx).

The Sale Water Park route (3 miles) starts at the car park, and leads around the perimeter of the lake to the River Mersey. This path comes closest to the visitor centre and facilities.

Another possibility is simply to walk down to the river, and follow the riverbank path for as long as you want. Dogs are discouraged from the Priory Gardens Trail to protect nesting birds.

Facilities

Free car park. WC. Café. Picnic area. Campervan access.

Clifton Country Park M27 6NG   Southbound only

Getting there
From Junction 16 turn right, A666, Kearsley. Continue to a brown
tourist sign for Clifton Country Park and turn right, Clifton House Road.
Turn right at the next sign to the car park.

Return to M60 southbound
Leave the car park and turn left at the crossroads. At the T-junction
turn right, A666. Enter Kearsley and continue on the A666 Bolton. At
a roundabout, take exit 1 to join the M61 (Salford, Manchester, M60).
Towards Junction 1 move into the right-hand lane. Follow signs to
Liverpool and Birmingham to merge onto the M60 southbound.

The walk
Clifton Country Park, set in the Irwell Valley, is a haven of calm with air
pungent with the scent of wild flowers in summer.
    There are several trails. The Perimeter Trail (easy) is 2.5km, the
Wet Earth Trail 3.5km, and the Lake Trail 4.5km.
    The path circling the lake is hard-surfaced and accessible to
wheelchair users.

Facilities
Free gated car park 0930 to dusk. Visitor centre open irregularly. WC
(visitor centre hours). Children's play area. Campervan access.

Getting there

From Junction 19 take the A576, Manchester City Centre and Heaton Hall and Park, eastbound exit 3, westbound exit 1. Turn right at the traffic lights, A6044. Enter Prestwich and turn right, signed Lakes car park.

Return to M60 Junction 19

Exit the park grounds and turn left. At the traffic lights turn left A576, Rochdale road. Continue to return to the M60.

The walk

With 600 acres of parkland, Heaton Park is a massively popular open space with Mancunians as the huge car park suggests. As this is also a venue for large-scale, open-air concerts and events, the road-weary hound may despair of a tree and piece of ground to call his own amongst all the municipal merry-making during the school holidays.

For a quiet stroll, walk round the edge of the lake to reach the Hall and facilities. Continue to the front of the Hall to find an open area where the doggie people are. There is plenty of space here to relax and take in the view of Manchester and the Pennines beyond.

Facilities

Free car park, closes at dusk. WC+disabled. Cafés. Visitor centre. Children's play areas, pets corner and show farm. Rowing boat hire. Tram museum. Garden centre. Campervan access.

Alkrington Woods   Eastbound only

Getting there

From Junction 20 turn left, A644, Middleton. Enter Middleton. At the next two roundabouts take exit 1, A576 Bury. Alkrington Woods car park is signed to the left. Alternative parking is in a lay-by further along on the left, with direct access to the woods.

Return to M60 eastbound

Turn right from the car park, A576. At the roundabout continue A576 Oldham direction. At the next roundabout take exit 3, A664 Manchester. At the traffic lights turn left, M60 Oldham. At the next roundabout take exit 3, M60. Enter Chadderton. Turn left at the traffic lights, M60. Turn right onto the M60 where signed.

The walk

Alkrington Woods is a local nature reserve occupying the grounds of the former Alkrington Hall Estate. Several marked and graded trails encourage walkers to meander through the woodland.

There are two easy, all-access, 1.5 mile routes with white or blue posts; a medium, 1.5 mile route with yellow posts, and a 3.5 mile route marked in red.

Facilities

Free car parking. Information board with trail routes. Picnic tables. Campervan access.

motorway walks for drivers and dogs

Daisy Nook Country Park OL7 9JY

Getting there

From Junction 23 follow signs for the A635, Ashton-under-Lyne. Enter Ashton-under-Lyne. At a roundabout take exit 1 Oldham. At the traffic lights, turn left A627, Oldham Road. At the next traffic lights turn left, Newmarket Road. Turn right, signed Daisy Nook Garden Centre, and the entrance to the park is on the right.

Return to M60 Junction 23

Leave the car park and turn left. At the T-junction turn left, A627 Ashton-under-Lyne. At the traffic lights turn right, signed M60, to follow signs back to the motorway.

The walk

This is a gem of a walk. There are so many paths that it must be possible to visit Daisy Nook a hundred times and never repeat a route.

One of the main features is the Hollinwood Branch providing flat, level walking over a disused canal.

The Oldham Way and the Tameside Trail routes also go through the park.

Facilities

Free parking. Visitor centre. WC+disabled (visitor centre hours). Café. Shop. Children's play area. Picnic areas. Campervan access.

Reddish Vale Country Park SK5 7HE

Getting there

From Junction 24 take the A57, Manchester. Enter Denton, and turn left
at the traffic lights, Reddish Lane. Pass a station and enter Reddish.
After a Morrisons supermarket turn left at the lights into Reddish
Vale Road. Take the second entrance at the bottom of the hill, signed
Country Park.

Return to M60 Junction 24

Leave the park. At the traffic lights, turn right B6167, Reddish road.
Continue to traffic lights and turn right, A57 Barnsley to return to the
M60.

The walk

This is a wonderful walking park, and its wildness surprises, given that
it lies in the middle of urban Manchester and a tangle of motorways.
Once a calico and dye works, the transformation to rural wonder is
amazing.

There are a number of signed paths and routes through the park,
with full details available from the visitor centre. Walks start across the
bridge, and the paths are clear and well maintained.

Facilities

At the main entrance: free gated car park. WC+disabled. Visitor centre.
Picnic area. Mobility scooter loan from the visitor centre, call 0161
4775637 to book. Campervan
access.

Getting there

From Junction 27 take the A626, Marple. Turn left at the traffic lights – A626 Marple. Pass a Co-op supermarket, and turn left at traffic lights, Turncroft Lane. Park by the gates of the Vernon Museum Tea Rooms.

Return to M60 eastbound

Return down Turncroft Lane and at the traffic lights turn right into Hall Street. At the next set of traffic lights turn right, signed M60. At the roundabout take exit 5, signed M60 East, and rejoin the motorway.

The walk

There are two parks here, each with their own distinctive character. Dog walkers will prefer the 90-acre Woodbank Memorial Park, which is cut through by a number of trails, including the Fred Perry Way and the Valley Way. There's plenty of space here for off-lead walking, and it seems that the further you go, the better it gets. To reach the Memorial Park, turn right at the sign by the entrance gates.

By contrast, Vernon Park is immaculately manicured, with display flowerbeds and gracious lawns.

Facilities

Free parking, disabled spaces. Tea Room 1000-1600 daily. Trail pack for walkers available from the museum. Campervan access.

From Liverpool to Hull

Junction	
8	Clockface Colliery Country Park
9	Sankey Valley Park
11	Risley Moss Nature Reserve
21	Ogden Reservoir
22	Saddleworth Moor
27	Oakwell Hall
36	Airmyn

Getting there

From Junction 8, turn in the direction of Burtonwood. Enter Burtonwood. Turn left, unsigned, Gorsey Lane. Pass a farm on the right and continue to a sign for Clockface Colliery Country Park. The unsigned entrance is on the left.

Return to M62 Junction 8

Turn right out of the car park. At the T-junction turn right, Clay Lane. At the roundabout take exit 2 signed M62 and return to the motorway.

The walk

This country park is a fantastic piece of regeneration work, transforming a former colliery site into a peaceful and spacious environment.

Popular with dog walkers and horse riders, there are many paths to wander along for a highly enjoyable walk. The paths are clear and wide, and there's no danger of getting lost. A real stressbuster of a park!

Facilities

Free car park, with height restriction, open 0800 to dusk.

Sankey Valley Park WA5 9PB

Getting there
From Junction 9 take the A49, Warrington. At a roundabout take exit 2, A574 Widnes, and stay on the A574 Widnes road over successive roundabouts until signed to Sankey Valley Park. Turn right to enter the park at a brown tourist sign.

Return to M62 Junction 9
Leave the park and take exit 3 at the roundabout, A574. At the next roundabout take exit 3, signed M62/M6 and continue through the roundabouts following signs to the M62.

The walk
Sankey Valley Park, part of the Mersey Forest, is a seven mile linear park, successfully created from a disused railway and waste ground. The Sankey Canal runs through the park. There is an emphasis on family pursuits, with a pirate ship and maze for children.

Signed pathways run through the park, and there are many other paths, too. The canal path is ideal for dog walking and also forms part of the Trans-Pennine Trail. Once the choice is made to go left or right, navigation couldn't be simpler.

Facilities
Free car park. WC+disabled (not always open). Picnic area. Children's activities and play areas. Campervan access.

Getting there

From Junction 11 take the A574, Warrington, eastbound exit 4;
westbound exit 2. At a roundabout take exit 1, Risley Moss. At the next
roundabout take exit 2, Risley Moss, and enter the park from the next
roundabout.

Return to M62 Junction 11

Exit the car park and at the roundabout take exit 2, signed M6, M62,
Warrington. Continue straight at the next roundabout, and take exit 3 at
the next roundabout A574, Manchester. Continue on the A574 to return
to the M62.

The walk

There are over 200 acres of natural space to enjoy at Risley Moss, with
some well-signed trails, as well as the opportunity to wander off-path
and just soak up the atmosphere.

An easy-access path is fully accessible and 650m in length. The
Nature Trail is 1.6km long and leads through the trees on a well-
maintained path.

Risley Moss is a site of special scientific interest because its peat
has more or less survived industrialisation and marauding garden
centres, and a regeneration project is under way to 're-wet' the peat.

Facilities

Car park free, gated. Visitor centre. WC. Picnic tables. Campervan
access.

Ogden Reservoir OL16 3TD

Getting there
From Junction 21 take exit 2, A663, Shaw. Turn left, A640 Huddersfield. Turn left, Ogden Lane, signed The Bull's Head. Park in the car park opposite The Bull's Head.

Return to M62 Junction 21
Return down Ogden Lane and turn right at the T-junction. At the next junction turn right, Newhey Road, signed M62. Take exit 1 at a roundabout signed M62 and follow the signs to rejoin the motorway.

The walk
Turn left from the car park, and right up a lane (private road). Ahead and to the left you will see a green bank which forms the dam for Ogden Reservoir.

   Turn left at a yellow waymark arrow to go up some steps and across the top of the dam. At the other side of the dam, climb the steps and turn right. Go through a kissing gate and continue ahead through a leafy landscape. When the path forks, turn right to climb a small hill. Near the top, there's a track and access to moorland with the opportunity to ramble for hours.

Facilities
At The Bull's Head (01706 847992) food is served from midday. Closed Monday. Dogs allowed in the beer garden.

Getting there
From Junction 22 take the A672, Oldham. Immediately after a 50mph sign pull into the car parking area on the right-hand side.

Return to M62 Junction 22
Turn left out of the parking area and return to the M62.

The walk
This is part of the Pennine Way, so the scope for walking is limitless.

Cross the road and follow a gentle, uphill path through the moorland. The path is safe for off-lead dogs when you move away from the road, and there are wide open spaces to the left and right. Walk beyond the concrete trig point and turn around at a halfway point of your choosing.

There are also public footpath signs in the opposite direction.

Facilities
Free parking. Campervan access.

Oakwell Hall WF17 9LG

Getting there

From Junction 27 take the A62, Huddersfield. Pass the West Yorkshire retail park/Ikea and continue at the traffic lights, signed Oakwell Hall Museum. At the next traffic lights turn right, Oakwell Hall Museum. Pass a pub on the left, and turn right into Oakwell Hall Country Park. Park in the Bottom car park.

Return to M62 Junction 27

Turn left out of the car park (Bottom car park). At the traffic lights turn left, signed M62 East and West, and continue to rejoin the M62.

The walk

There are marked trails throughout the park, and detailed leaflets are available at the information point.

A well-planned system of paths makes the most of the 110 acres of the park. From the Bottom car park join the Nature Trail (2 miles) to get to the visitor centre and facilities.

The focal point of the park is the Elizabethan manor house, featured in ITV's *Wuthering Heights*. The house museum is out of bounds to dogs, but the café is dog-friendly and provides large dog water bowls.

Facilities

Two free car parks, height restricted. WC+disabled. Café. Information point. Shop. Children's adventure playground and interactive activities. Ranger service. Museum.

PUBLIC FOOTPATH RAWCLIFFE

PUBLIC FOOTPATH HOOK

Getting there
From Junction 36 take the A614, Rawcliffe. Turn right, signed Airmyn. Enter the village and park in The Percy Arms car park.

Return to M62 Junction 36
Turn left out of the car park, and then left again onto the A614 to return to the motorway.

The walk
Cross the lane in front of the pub, climb the steps to a broad, grassy pathway to the memorial, and bear off into a field. The River Aire is to the left. At the corner of the field it's possible to see where the Aire converges with the Ouse.

For a 40-50 minute walk, follow the path around the fields alongside the river until your halfway point, then turn around to return to The Percy Arms.

Facilities
At the 17th century Percy Arms (01405 780792) lunch is served 1200-1400 Mon-Sat, Sun 1200-1700. Well-behaved dogs on leads are allowed in the outdoor seating area; dog water is available.

Scotland

M8
Edinburgh to Greenock, via Glasgow
Junction
3	Beecraigs Country Park
5	Polkemmet Country Park

M9
Edinburgh to Stirling
Junction
2	Blackness Beach (southbound)
3	Linlithgow Palace (northbound)
5	Callendar Park (northbound)
9	Bannockburn

M74/A74M
Glasgow to Carlisle
Junction
5	Strathclyde Country Park
7	Chatelherault Country Park (southbound)
12	Castle Dangerous (northbound)
15	Moffat
17	Lockerbie Manor Hotel

18   Lochmaben Castle (northbound)
19   Brownmoor Wood

M77
Glasgow to Fenwick
Junction
2   Pollok House and Country Park

M90
Edinburgh to Perth
Junction
3   Pittencrieff Park
5   Lochore Meadows
6   Loch Leven
11   Scone Palace

walking THE DOG

Beecraigs Country Park EH49 6PL

Getting there
From Junction 3 take the A899, Bathgate, Broxburn. At the roundabout take exit 2, Dechmont A899, and at the next roundabout take exit 1, Dechmont. Turn right into Burnhouse Road, and continue for a mile. Turn left and pass Blackcraig Farm on the left, then North Mains farm on the right. Turn right to enter Beecraigs Country Park.

Return to M8 Junction 3
Exit Beecraigs and turn left. Pass the farms and turn right, Burnhouse Road. At the T-junction turn left, and at the roundabout take exit 2, A899, and continue to return to the M8.

The walk
With over 900 acres of grounds, there's a real variety of walking routes in this very active country park. Choose your walk at the visitor centre and buy the route leaflet.

Three marked trails start from the Balvormie car park (turn left from the visitor centre car park, turn left and then left again). These are waymarked with coloured posts.

The Balvormie overflow car park is 20m beyond the entrance to the car park proper on the right. Don't be fooled by an apparently locked gate; the entrance is further on.

Facilities
Free parking. WC. Visitor centre 0900-1600. Shop. Refreshments. Trail leaflets 20p each. Rangers on duty. Partial wheelchair/buggy routes from some access points. Children's adventure playground. Campervan access.

Getting there

From Junction 5 merge onto the B7057, signed Shotts, Harthill. At the T-junction turn left, B7066 Harthill. Enter Eastfield, pass a petrol station on the left, and enter West Lothian county. Turn left at the tourist sign for Polkemmet Country Park.

Return to M8 Junction 5

Turn right out of the park, and turn right signed M8. Continue ahead and turn right, B7057, to return to the M8.

The walk

This country park has been formed from the grounds of the Baillie Estate.

There's a good choice of routes to suit the needs of all walkers. The Red, Yellow and Blue routes are all under 2 miles, and the Green route is longer at just over 3 miles. There are also plenty of smaller paths to wander off on.

The Red and Blue routes start from the left of the car park entrance, and the Yellow and Green routes from just before the entrance to the car park.

As an extension to the Red and Blue trails, visit 'the Horn;' a music sculpture commission to liven the view across the M8.

Facilities

Free parking. WC. Children's playground and a steam train engine. Picnic tables and BBQ area. The children's 'Fantasy Forest' is off-limits to dogs. Campervan access.

walking THE DOG

Blackness Beach EH49 7NG   Southbound only

Getting there

From Junction 2 turn left, B8035, Forth
Road Bridge. At a T-junction turn left,
A904, Bo'ness and Blackness Castle.
Turn right at a tourist sign to Blackness
Castle. At a T-junction turn right and enter
Blackness village. Turn left at the car park
sign in the village and park in the seafront car park.

Return to M9 Southbound

Leave the village on the B903, Linlithgow. At the T-junction turn left,
A803, and continue to return to the M9 southbound.

The walk

Walk from the car park towards Blackness Castle and turn right at a
footpath sign next to a dog-waste bin. This is signed Chapel, and is a
short circular walk route across headland meadows to the right of the
castle complex. It's a good space for dogs and there's a grand view over
the estuary to the Forth Bridge.

In fine weather a second option is to walk along the beach, away
from the castle.

Blackness Castle, sitting squat and solid on its promontory, is
mainly 16th century.

Facilities

At beach: free parking. WC. Campervan access. At Blackness Castle:
WC. Visitor centre. Visitors' car park. Dogs on leads in courtyard only.

Getting there

From Junction 3 turn left, A803, Linlithgow. Enter Linlithgow and at the roundabout take exit 2, A803, Falkirk, Stirling and Linlithgow Palace. In the town centre turn right to Linlithgow Palace and car park.

Return to M9 northbound

Exit Linlithgow Palace and turn right onto the A803. At the roundabout take exit 2 A803 and continue ahead to return to the M9.

The walk

For a short stroll, walk down the grassy slopes of the hill from the gatehouse, where there are several paths leading down to Linlithgow Loch. Turn right at the water and then amble around the base of the palace to return up the slope from the rear of the palace.

For a longer walk, follow the path down to the loch to a signed path around it.

The prosperous little town of Linlithgow has plenty of cafes and restaurants.

Facilities

Free parking. WC. Palace museum. Tesco on the A803 roundabout for picnic supplies.

Callendar Park FK1 1YR   Northbound only

Getting there

From Junction 5 take exit 1 and follow signs to Falkirk, A9. At Bog Roundabout take exit 1, A905, and at Mary Street roundabout take exit 3, Falkirk, A803. At the next roundabout turn left, Callendar House, and then right, signed Callendar Park, for the car park.

Return to M9 northbound

Leave the car park and cross the roundabout, signed M9. At the traffic lights turn right, signed M9. At the next roundabout continue ahead. Follow the signs for M9 Grangemouth to return to the M9 northbound.

The walk

First appearances suggest that this is just a popular family park, where walkers and dogs take their chances with the youngsters enjoying the play facilities.

For a calm, 40 minute walk aim for the lake, with the towers of Callendar House on the left, and make a circular tour of the lake, through a large area of stately parkland. Small paths lead off into light-dappled woodland, and dogs can run freely.

Facilities

Free car park. WC+disabled. Refreshments, kiosk for snacks, picnic tables. Children's play areas and swan pedaloes for hire on the lake. Dog poo bags available free from kiosk. Campervan access.

motorway walks for drivers and dogs

Bannockburn FK7 0LJ

Getting there

From Junction 9 follow the A872, Stirling; northbound exit 5,
southbound exit 1. Follow the brown tourist signs to the Bannockburn
Heritage Centre. The car park is on the left-hand side, and clearly
signed.

Return to M9 Junction 9

Turn right out of the car park, and follow signs to the M9.

The walk

If you first watch the bloodthirsty performance by the actor/warrior in
the visitor centre, the Bannockburn battlefield may be something of an
anti-climax.

But your dog won't mind that the open land here is more playing
field than ghost-filled museum, as it's an ideal space for a bound with
the hound, or for young visitors brandishing swords.

Facilities

Free car park. Visitor centre 1000-1730 March-Oct, WC+disabled. Shop.
Exhibition and exciting battle video. Campervan access.

Refreshments: motorway services at Junction 9; Klondike
Garden Centre for coffee and cakes on the left before the entrance to
Bannockburn, or the King Robert Hotel Bistro next to the battle site.

walking THE DOG

Strathclyde Country Park ML1 3RT

Getting there
From Junction 5 follow the tourist sign for Strathclyde Country Park.
There are a number of car parks inside the park, all on the right-hand
side.

Return to M74 Junction 5 or 6
Northbound return to Junction 5: turn left from the car park and leave
the park, continuing directly back to the M74 as signed. Southbound
return to Junction 6: turn right out of the car park and continue. At a
crossroads turn right, drive over the river and follow signs to return to
the M74 southbound.

The walk
Foreshaw beach, at the first car park, is popular with families, and gives
access to a grassy lakeside beach, children's playground, WC, and an
ice-cream van in summer.

Scotland's first theme park, with cafes and children's
entertainment, is on the left just before the second car park.

More rural walks begin from the third and fourth car parks, where
a number of trails lead down to the lakeside. A circular path is hard-
surfaced, and accessible.

Facilities
Free parking. Campervan access. Meals available at the Toby Carvery (in
the Express Holiday Inn) just before the exit for M74 Junction 5.

Getting there
Leave the M74 at Junction 7 and turn right, Larkhall, A72. Turn left at traffic lights, signed Chatelherault Country Park.

Return to M74 southbound
Exit Chatelherault and turn left, A72. Continue until a right turn onto the A723. Follow signs to return to the M74 southbound.

The walk
There are six signed trails of different lengths around this 500 acre country park, and free leaflets for the 10 miles of trails can be picked up at the visitor centre. The Cadzow Oaks trail is one of the shorter walks, and The Riccarton Path is the longest of them all.

There is plenty of space at this fantastic park, and it's an ideal stopping point before heading into the city.

Facilities
Free parking. WC+disabled, café. First aid point. Exhibits and visitor centre. Children's adventure playground. Accessible paths. Big buckets of dog water. Campervan access.

Larkhall town has bakeries, several supermarkets, and grocers for picnic provisions.

walking THE DOG

Castle Dangerous   Northbound only

Getting there
From Junction 12 take the A70, Ayr.
Enter Douglas. Turn right at a brown
sign to the Cameronian monument.
Pass St Brides Church on the left,
and park in a bay on the right
opposite some cottages.

Return to M74 northbound
Turn around and return along Main
Street. Turn left at the T-junction and
continue over a mini roundabout.
At the roundabout take exit 1, A70,
Edinburgh. At the next roundabout
take exit 1, Glasgow, M74.

The walk
Leave the parking area and follow
the black footpath arrow along the
track to Castle Dangerous, past a
lake on the left. Return the same
way.
     A number of castles which have
inhabited this site have endured
brutal and gory pasts defending the
route to the Clyde Valley, and the
Heritage Centre in the town has the
full details.

Facilities
Free parking. Campervan access.
Picnic tables on the walk route.
Hard tarmac path (after cattle grid).
Children's playground in park below
church. Shops in the town for picnic
supplies, and petrol station.

Getting there

From Junction 15 follow signs to Moffat, A701. Enter Moffat and park in the first car park on the left.

Return to A74(M) Junction 15

Turn right out of the car park, and continue on the A701 to rejoin the motorway.

The walk

Branded as the first 'Walkers' Town' in Scotland, some real passion has gone into creating walking trails in and around Moffat.

Trails start at the car park and include a 2 mile walk to Chapel, and a Woodside walk at around 3 miles.

Many paths are hard-surfaced, and fully accessible to wheelchairs and buggies.

Longer routes include woodland walks (Gallowhill), and a forest walk in Craigieburn (just over 6 miles). One walk may have dog restrictions due to cattle grazing. There are many more walks, and a walking festival in October.

Facilities

Free parking. WC. Board with walking trail routes. Shops for picnic supplies. Campervan access.

Meals served at The Black Bull Hotel (01683 220206; DG10 9EG), and The Buccleigh Arms Hotel (01683 220003; DG10 9ET). Well-behaved dogs are welcome in both hotels.

Lockerbie Manor Hotel DG11 2RG

Getting there
From Junction 17 follow signs for Lockerbie, B7068. At the next roundabout take the Lockerbie B7068 exit and turn left. At a T-junction turn left, and then right to park at the Lockerbie Manor Hotel (patrons only).

Return to A74(M) Junction 17
Turn left at the end of the hotel drive. Take the first right turn, unsigned. Cross a light-controlled bridge, and then turn right at a T-junction. Thereafter, the A74(M) is signed.

The walk
This walk lies within the extensive grounds of the hotel, and is a safe space for children and dogs to let off steam.

Walk slightly downhill with the hotel to your left. Go through a gate, ignoring a path to the right. Turn right at the path junction and then right onto a narrower path before a white cottage. The path seems overgrown at this point, but opens out past a 5-bar gate to cross a stream. Continue uphill for a while, turning around at a suitable point to return to the hotel.

Facilities
At the Lockerbie Manor Hotel (01576 202610) coffee, meals, and tea are served in old-style, relaxing comfort. Well-behaved dogs on leads are permitted in the lounge; dog water provided. Campervan access.

Getting there
From Junction 18 turn right B723, Lockerbie. Bear left, B7076, and take exit 2 at a roundabout. Turn right, Lockerbie, and at a T-junction turn right, Lochmaben, A709. Enter Lochmaben and turn left, Dalton B7020. Turn left signed Lochmaben Castle and park by the castle ruins.

Return to A74(M) northbound
Leave the castle and turn right at the end of the track. Enter Lochmaben and turn right at the T-junction, signed A709 Lockerbie. Turn left, signed A74(M), and then right at the next roundabout. Follow the signs back to the A74(M) North.

The walk
For a shortish walk, take the grassy path running anti-clockwise around the lake.

Close by the castle is a small 'beach,' ideal for dog swimming, and also with picnic tables. Longer walks are signed from the track to the castle, and indicated with green pointers.

The castle has seen a lot of action over the centuries. It was owned at one time by the Brus family, ancestors of the famous Scottish King, Robert the Bruce.

Facilities
Free parking. Picnic tables.

Brownmoor Wood

Getting there
From Junction 19 take the B725, Ecclefechan, exit 1 at the roundabout.
At the next roundabout, take exit 1 Ecclefechan, B7076. Turn right onto
a minor road and pass the entrance to the Cressfield Caravan Park.
Continue to the end and park.

Return to A74(M)
Retrace your route along the minor road and turn left. At a roundabout
take exit 2, A74(M), and return to the motorway.

The walk
Walk past a bungalow to a clear path and through three swing gates
towards the woodland ahead. Pass a Brownmoor Wood Forestry
Commission sign, and stay on the path as it winds gently uphill. After
100m or so there's a clearing, and the start point of two marked circular
trails in the forest; colour-coded red and blue. The paths are well
maintained and easy to follow.

The essayist and historian Thomas Carlyle was born and raised
in Ecclefechan. He was buried in the churchyard here, after refusing a
berth at Westminster Abbey.

Facilities
Free parking. Picnic tables. Campervan access. Public WC in
Ecclefechan.

Getting there

From Junction 2 follow the sign for Pollokshaws B762. At the Round Toll roundabout take exit 1 Pollokshaws, B769. Follow the B769 and turn left at a sign for Pollok House and Country Park. The car park is just after the entrance to Pollok House.

Return to M77 Junction 2

Follow the one-way system to leave the park at the Dumbreck Road exit. Turn right onto the B769. At the Round Toll roundabout take exit 3 signed M77, and return to the motorway.

The walk

A marked trail explores the 360 acres of parkland, and some of the historical, natural and man-made features of the park.

There's a small area surrounding the house where dogs must be on leads, but otherwise the grounds are open to unfettered canine exploration. Highland cattle live in the grounds, and wise walkers will avoid upsetting them ...

Facilities

P&D car park. Disabled parking places outside Pollok house museum. WC+disabled in Old Stable Yard and Burrell Collection. Tea rooms, Children's play area. Dog water. Full access to house and park for disabled visitors. Campervan access.

Pittencrieff Park KY12 8QH

Getting there
From Junction
3 take the A907, W
Dunfermline.
Pass a football
ground. At the next
roundabout take
the A907, Stirling,
Pittencrieff Park.
Turn left, signed
Tourist Information,
and park in the Glenbridge short stay car park on the left. 3 m

Return to M90 Junction 3
Leave the car park and turn right at the traffic lights. Carry straight on
to rejoin the M90.

The walk
Follow the blue signs to enter Pittencrieff Park. Inside the park marked
trails meander through its 76 acres, past formal gardens, an ornamental
waterfall, and a museum.

Other visitor attractions are
near the park gates on the other
side of the park.

Facilities
P&D car park. Campervan
access. In Pittencrieff Park:
WC+disabled. Restaurant. Hard-
surface paths. Dog exercise
area. Children's play areas.

In Dunfermline: Cafés,
restaurants and pubs, many
with outdoor seating. Plenty
of bakeries and delis for picnic
supplies.

Getting there

Follow signs to Glenrothes, B9097. At a T-junction turn right, B966, Cowden Heath. Turn left, Ballingry, Lochore. Enter Ballingry. Turn right at a T-junction. Enter Crosshill. Turn right, signed Lochore Meadows Country Park. The car park is at the end of the lane.

Return to M90 Junction 5

Leave the park, turn left at the mini roundabout. Turn left, Ballingry Road and at the T-junction turn left. Turn right, B996, then left, B9097, to return to the M90.

The walk

There are four marked trails in this extensive country park.

The Golden Triangle walk is wheelchair-accessible, and is a mile-long, hard path to and from a castle.

A three-mile circular path around the loch is also hard-surfaced.

The third trail is an uphill track to Harran Woods, and the final option – 'The Pit Road' – is a three-mile flat path winding around the headstocks of a former coal mine. Other woodland paths are signed in red.

Dogs should be taken to use the dog loop, a short, circular path which gives an opportunity for defecation before starting a walk.

Facilities

Free parking. WC+disabled. Visitor centre 0900-1600. Also WCs at the Outdoor Centre when the visitor centre is closed. Café. Ranger service. Children's play area, boats and a small beach for families (no dogs on the beach). Campervan access.

Loch Leven KY13 8UF

Getting there
From Junction 6 take the A977, Kinross. Continue to the B918 (Station
Road) and turn right at a mini roundabout. Turn left at a sign to
Lochleven Castle, and follow signs for the castle through a residential
area, and then park near the
Boathouse Bistro.

Return to M90 Junction 6
Turn right at the end of
Burns Begg Street. At a mini
roundabout turn left, Station
Road, and return to the M90.

The walk
Take the ducted path
opposite the Bistro to the
Loch Leven nature reserve.
Kids will probably head off to
the pirate playground on the
left, whilst keen swimming
hounds will be equally intent
on getting to one of the
lochside dog beaches. The
path follows a line of sight
to the trees and the small
promontory directly ahead,
just under a mile.

Boats go to the
Lochleven island castle,
where Mary Queen of Scots
was once a 'guest.'

Facilities
Free car park. WC.
Picnic tables at the park.
Campervan access. Meals are available all day at the Boathouse Bistro
(01577 865386).

Scone Palace PH2 6BD

Getting there

From Junction 11 take the A85, Perth. Enter Perth and follow signs to Blairgowrie. Turn left, A93, Blairgowrie and Scone Palace. Turn left into Scone Palace where signed.

Return to M90 Junction 11

Leave the palace grounds and turn right. Continue at the traffic lights, and follow the blue signs to return to the M90.

The walk

A grand location for a walk, combining a visit to one of Scotland's premier visitor spots with fun activities for kids, historical viewing, a fine coffee shop, tasteful souvenir shopping, and dog happiness, too!

Turn right to pass through the gateway opposite the palace, which will bring you into The Wild Garden and Pinetum, ideal for a short walk where dogs can run off-lead.

Facilities

Grounds entry charge. Open 0930-1700, Apr-Oct. WC+disabled. Shop, restaurant and café with outdoor seating. Children's activities. House, gallery, museum. Dog water at café. Campervan access.

Walk Notes

Motorway	Junction	Name	Comments

Walk Notes

Motorway	Junction	Name	Comments

Walk Notes

Motorway	Junction	Name	Comments

Walk Notes

Motorway	Junction	Name	Comments

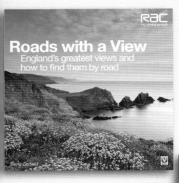
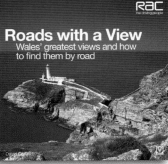
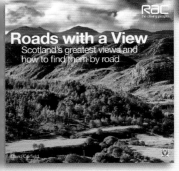